DEDICATION

This book is dedicated my parents and my lovely wife and to the many security professionals who daily work to ensure the safety of our nation's critical infrastructures. We want to recognize the thousands of dedicated individuals who strive to protect our national assets but who seldom receive praise and often are only noticed when an incident occurs. To you, we say thank you for a job well done!

ABOUT THIS BOOK

 Important Technology Skills

Information technology (IT) offers many career paths and information security is one of the fastest-growing tracks for IT professionals. This book provides coverage of the materials you need to begin your exploration of information security. In addition to covering all of the CompTIA Security+ exam objectives, additional material is included to help you build a solid introductory knowledge of information security.

Table of Contents

Chapter 1: Information privacy and security

Chapter 2: Identification & authentication

Chapter 3: Software program security

Chapter 4: Malicious code

Chapter 5: Interception and Access

Chapter 6: Encryption

CHAPTER 1

INFORMATION PRIVACY AND SECURITY

I wanted to pose an interesting philosophical question namely why is information security necessary.

PC security, otherwise called digital security or IT security is the assurance of PC frameworks from the robbery or harm to the equipment, programming or the data on them, and also from disturbance or confusion of the administrations they give.

Although many of the Investments that are made into information privacy and security are not related to malicious attacks. There is nevertheless an extraordinarily large amount of investment in information privacy and security mechanisms that are targeted toward protecting systems against attacks by malicious parties from a philosophical perspective.

It's important to consider what this says about Trinity on the one hand it shows that we are certainly curious creatures but on the other hand. It shows that we as a species are not particularly trustworthy and we're all so greedy there are many people in the organizations of the Toronto and even governments in the world that would be very happy to steal personal private information from you or your organization for their own gain.

This appears to be a natural trait of human beings in virtually all cultures and it's important to note that if we were not like this as the quantity of time money and other resources that individuals organizations and government must invest into protecting their information assets would be much less than I was today with those philosophical thoughts.

Information security is characterized by interactions with technology computational capabilities are being embedded in a rapidly increasing number and variety of products anything from athletic house to kitchen appliances to implantable medical devices and what does it means is that with every passing day computers are controlling and administering and making decisions about more and more aspects of Our Lives. What we can conclude from the situation is that we are becoming more and more dependent on these information. and community colleges every single day and this situation has very important implications with respect to our privacy and security to better understand why consider the relationship between our two islands on technology and risk. because we live in a world where we are increasingly entrusting our wives and our livelihoods to computer Technologies and because those Technologies are not entirely Dependable safe or secure our increasing Reliance on these information and communication Technologies brings with it a great deal of new risks.

WHY ENTER INFORMATION SECURITY?

 PROS

Entering the world of cyber security has A LOT of benefits! These are just a few...

Tangibles
- Growing and stable profession
- Workforce shortages persist
- High salaries
- Mission critical roles

Intangibles
- A consistent and evolving challenge
- Define your own career
- Geographic leniency
- Be the hit of the party: "I'm a hacker!"

That were not present prior to the rise of the information age as a disciplined mind as a profession then one of the major goals of Information Security is to find ways of mitigating these risks that is to allow us to have our cake and eat it too. Although many people of the world of information privacy and security has one characterized Find hacker's cyber terrorists or government-sponsored information. as well in reality the scope of information privacy and security is much broader turn around one way of understanding the breadth of the scope is to consider information security from the perspective of it failures our modern Information Technology fail for many different reasons first considered physical failures. These are Hardware devices turn on Hardware can and does fail even in the modern era many of our traditional Technologies still rely on moving parts and a failure of any of these moving Parts in Cascade to cause a wide array of the information technology. As a whole other electronic components can fail and when these components failed permanently the cause of the problem is much easier to diagnose than when they fail intermittently.

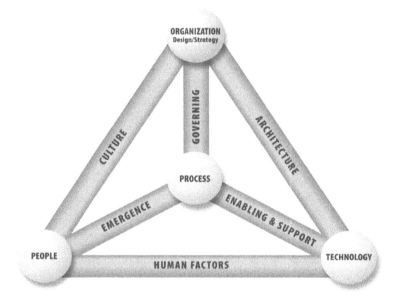

It is therefore important for managers and system administrators not only to expect that their physical it devices will fail but also to develop plans for how to address those failures. When they inevitably occur beyond physical failures we have other types of Information Technology failures as well and bees can best be understood by considering the intersection of two different dimensions. a long one to mention we have a spectrum which ranges from malicious two non-malicious that is the source of the failure is caused intentionally or unintentionally. and along the other dimension we have a spectrum which ranges from harmless to catastrophic putting these two Dimensions against each other provides us with a geometric space in which we can easily classify our non-physical Information Technology failures a failure than my own non-malicious and harmless it might be non-religious but catastrophic it might be malicious.

But caused no harm or the worst scenario it may be a malicious attack. That cause's catastrophic damage to our information a smile again remember that information security has a broad scope. And information security addresses each of these different types of failures what's more information security throughout failures. that have never before been seen or do not currently exist and that statement speaks to the dynamism and constant change that characterizes the world of information security so when thinking about information security remember that it has a vast scope we're talking here about protecting anything from tiny little room to graded circuits. All the way up massive clusters of servers that may involve thousands of unique machines were talking about protecting a local private Network that you may have in your home or your apartment all the way up to massive wide area networks or even the entire internet were talking about protecting Hardware, software, operating systems, databases, networks etc.

The scope of inquiry in computer security is vast continuously changing and ever-growing broadly speaking however computer security as being concerned Toronto protecting information assets and when we say information assets are over referring to is elements of the information system. that have value since value lies at the core of our focus our information security efforts a critical first step is identifying what within our organization has value and to, whom do those items. Information Technology assets is to subdivide assets into three categories.

First we have Hardware assets and these Kenwood Computing systems mobile devices networks and Communications channels. And we have software assets these can include operating systems off the shelf application programs mobile apps as well as custom or customized application programs. Finally we have data assets these are our files are databases the information that we generate in our daily lives or in carrying out our house. And as we will see it is often this class of assets that has the greatest value of all when considering this diagram.

Remember that the perceived value of an atom depends in part upon the ease with which that can be replaced certain components of an information system. Turn on the Jets Hardware mobile devices operating systems off-the-shelf software can be easily replaced by contrast custom applications or mobile apps and our data are often unique and irreplaceable. perhaps you can think of an example to our own your own life where you or someone you've known has lost say a laptop computer or mobile device many tiles they are upset not so much about the loss of the physical device the physical Hardware, itself but more so about the photos the course documents they needed they had for work etc. it is those files those data items that represent much of the value of a system to its Users can understand intuitively. Through examples such as this why the value of an asset often depends upon the eastern and we were able to replace that asset earlier.

We said that one of the major goals of information security was to mitigate security risks to another major goal of information security as a discipline and as a profession is not right to protect our valuable information assets and in order to approach the study of methods of protecting these assets .we will adopt what's known as a vulnerability threat control framework to begin considered a vulnerability this is a weakness in some aspect of an information system to know if a vulnerability is exploited and has the potential to cause lost her arm and a human being who intentionally exploit the vulnerability is perpetrating an attack on the system so an attack then tomorrow we need to find as an intentional exploitation of a system vulnerability.

Next we can consider a threat now the threat is simply a set of circumstances that has the potential to cause loss or harm and as we will see. You shortly threats and vulnerabilities are very closely related.

Finally we have controls and a control is something that we do or something that we have which helps to eliminate or reduce the vulnerability, another name for a control is a countermeasure now many people. when they are first learning about information security become confused than ever it's between a threat of vulnerability and control so let see a simple example, that I hope will help you to remember the difference between these products and then that you are walking over a bridge whenever you walk over a bridge.

There is always a threat to your safety namely that the bridge might collapse underneath you, so the possibility of the bridge collapsing he's a threat to your safety now if there is a weakness in the bridge say that there is a crack in the cement or the mortar between the blocks of Stone from which the bridge is constructed has begun to crumble or deteriorate. We don't know his weaknesses or vulnerabilities and if those vulnerabilities were to be exploited, the threat of the bridge collapsing would be actualized. And that might really cause you physical harm or control them is something that we do or something which helps us to eliminate or reduce the vulnerability. In this example we might apply bracing to reinforce the bridge or we may try to repair the cracks in the concrete thus reducing the possibility that the vulnerability will be exploited to Broadway.

Then threats are blocked 4 Mile from being actualized by controlling vulnerabilities .threats and what has come to be known as CIA that is confidentiality and availability. This Acronym CIA and the concepts for which it stands is commonly referred to as the security Triad. And we can think about threats as interfering with the confidentiality Integrity or availability to automation system confidentiality then is simply the ability of a system to ensure total assets are viewable or accessible only by authorized parties Integrity by contrast is the ability of a system to ensure that assets are modifiable or changeable only one authorized parties. And finally availability refers to the ability of a system to ensure that assets are usable by and accessible to all authorized parties confidentiality integrity and availability.

Then can also be seen as goals or objective of information security. Since together they represent three very desirable properties of an information system. While the sea Maritime has been around for many decades more recently. Other desirable system properties have also been identified and these are authentication non-repudiation and auditability with respect to the first two of these that has authentication and non-repudiation.

We are speaking here of systems that allow for communication or messaging with other systems or other users and in this regard authentication refers to the ability of a system to confirm the identity of sender. For example if you receive a message from your manager which instructs you to immediately stop working on the project tomorrow. You have been working on for the past year and turn your attention to another project you.

As the receiver of that message would like to be able to confirm the identity of the sender that is you would like to know how truly your boss who sent that message to you was. On the other side of this is non-repudiation and this is a property of a system in which a sender not convincingly deny, having sent a message returning to our previous example. If you received such a message from your manager instructing you to immediately discontinue working on a project. And if we assume that you are manager genuinely did send that message a desirable problem with system from your perspective would be to ensure that your manager could not deny having sent that message.

Finally have the ability as a desirable system property and this is simply the ability of a solid to trace all actions that are related to a given asset that way. If something goes wrong in the future we can trace backward through time and determine who did what in order to ensure that responsible parties are held to account. Harmful Acts no harm to my house to an information system in four General ways threw interception. For example, I like intercept valuable information flowing over a network Interruption. For example I might disrupt the information systems ability to carry out its tasks Toronto. Toronto location in which I might seek to modify an information system or modify its information assets.

Without being properly authorized to do so and Fabrication. In which we might try that create an identity. Or we might fabricate new information assets for the purpose of doing harm to the system as a whole each of these four acts is a harmful act through. Because it can affect A System's ability to ensure confidentiality Integrity or availability. Some additional details about confidentiality integrity and available beginning the First with confidentiality.

When it comes to confidentiality of good information security strategy is to adopt a need-to-know basis for determining who has access to data. And when they have access to those data essentially the idea here is that by default the user of a system should not have access to anything and that the information assets or capabilities that they are given with respect to the system are done. So only on a need-to-know basis that is we sure about system users information workers with all of the information assets that they need to do their jobs effectively and nothing more. Another interesting considering with respect to confidentiality is the question of how do we know if a user is the person or the system that they claim? Speaks directly to the difference between identification and Authentication. We can think of identification as the process of proving that someone is who they say they are by contrast.

We can think of authentication as the process of proving that something is genuine or true or authentic child in the world of information security.

It is often very difficult or impossible to truly identify a real human being or a specific system. Instead we commonly used methods of authentication rather than identification. And we assume that the credentials being used for Authentication are being used only by the real world human being or system to whom those credentials apply. This is of course it risky assumption since through to ashes or not malicious means. It might be very possible for me to obtain your login information and your problem. And if I were them to use that information to login to say your social networking account. As far as the social networking site is concerned I am you are writing your credentials the system is assuming, that I am not human being to whom those credentials belong similar to the need-to-know policy for data access to physical assets. Such as the server room or the network closet should also be granted only on a need-to-know basis confidentiality. Then is difficult to ensure with 100% certainty, but it is often the easiest to assess in terms of whether or not our efforts at confidentiality have been successful.

When thinking about the difference between confidentiality and integrity just remember, that confidentiality is concerned with access to information assets where is integrity is concerned with preventing unauthorized modification of assets to Integrity of course is more difficult to measure than confidentiality. Because it is context-dependent it means different things in different situations and what's more there are degrees of internal for these reasons.

Relationship Between Inherent Risk Profile and Cybersecurity Maturity Domains

Risk/Maturity Relationship		Inherent Risk Levels				
		Least	Minimal	Moderate	Significant	Most
Cybersecurity Maturity Level for Each Domain	Innovative					
	Advanced					
	Intermediate					
	Evolving					
	Baseline					

SOURCE: FEDERAL FINANCIAL INSTITUTIONS EXAMINATION COUNCIL (FFIEC)

It's necessary for each organization to establish its own criteria by which in Tech Liberty can be measured in advance with Integrity availability is also context-dependent. And this makes it a very complex issue put another way availability means different things to different people to a CEO. For example availability might mean can I access my corporate email from home to a data analyst availability might mean, we can carry out my analyses in a timely manner. Without having to wait turn on acceptable long period of time in order for the system to process my request as a general set of guidelines.

Then we might consider an asset to be available when there is a timely request response Fair allocation of resources fault tolerance built into the system .ease-of-use Turner and a good concurrency control strategy in place in order to address situations, in which multiple users are attempting to use the same as that at the same time summarization of threats. Then consider that threats can be caused by some natural event such as a fire a power failure and earthquake. A Mudslide, a tornado and a hurricane Etc or by human causes that is caused by something that a human being has done. In the case of a human-caused threat, the intention of the human might be benign tumor. Or it might be malicious. As examples of benign or non malicious intent, we can consider a situation in which harm is caused through a simple human error or perhaps someone turns over a power cord or accidentally delete an important file. These are all the time that is actualized through a benign or non-malicious intent. When there is malicious intent however that is when a human being is intending to cause harm we can then classify that malicious intent to another random or directed. and the difference between random or directed, malicious attacks is simply whether the attacker is targeting a specific organization individual or entity is a specific time is under intentional attack.

Then we can classify that as a directed malicious attack otherwise if an attacker engages in a malicious attack. And they do so without the intention of harming a specific organization and Tootsie or individual. Then we can classify that as a random malicious attack. Who then are these attackers trying to compromise the confidentiality Integrity or availability of our information systems turned out well. Surprisingly many attackers are simple amateurs, they act opportunistically.

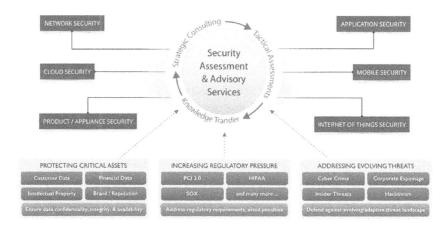

For example perhaps they find someone's lost mobile device for laptop computer and they decided to look through the files on that computer or perhaps. They are script kiddies or one of the hackers who find hacking tools on the same website. That they apply to their home computers or the computers at their school their place of work but outside of amateurs. We also have hackers and crackers with the difference here being that hackers.

Generally our attackers who have a non malicious intent they like to break into systems and look around to break into a system just to prove that they can do it. Where is a cracker by contrast has a moment they're breaking into a system with the goal of causing harm stealing data from the confidentiality, availability or Integrity of the system among these crackers you may have your criminals organized crime syndicates. Who seek to engage in malicious branches of information security for the purpose of financial or other gain two or more recently we've seen the rise of cyber terrorists who are not necessarily affiliated with a particular state government but never-the-less are conducting In support of some ideological and political agenda and of course we have state-supported information Warriors and Spas most modern countries including powerful countries.

Like all states in China employed vast armies of information Warriors. Whose job it is to try to spy on the government's role in Terry organizations of other countries. And collect intelligence through digital means. What's more this is no longer just a minor consideration in the United States for example the Department of Defense.

Increased size, scope and complexity of quality management requirements

Now considers cyberspace to be the fifth Battlefield the first for being land sea air and space and now cyberspace is considered the fifth Battlefield and a substantial amount of the nation's defense assets are being invested in efforts aimed at ensuring the nation's information superiority in cyberspace earlier we talked about the four types of Acts that can cause harm to an information system. Now harm its self-harm refers to the negative consequences. That can arise from an actualized threat. That is already in the system were to be exploited such that a threat became a reality what would be the implications of that actualized threat. This is a very difficult question to answer because the quantity or the amount of harm. That has sustained from a successful attack is often a subjective matter different people and different organizations will assign different values to their information technology assets. And with different values assigned to the same assets and identical attack to only perceive as causing a different amount of harm to two different organizations what's more the value of money information assets can change over time.

Consider for example the value of the transactions that your bank maintains for your checking account. If a malicious attack was launched against your bank. And the attackers were able to successfully to read or modify the transactions for your checking account. That took place in the last few days. Then we would almost certainly. Consider that act to a cause more harm to damage then if the same attackers had modified transaction data for your account where the transactions were 8 or 10 years old. This situation speaks to the relationship between the values of information time. Most modern information scientists believe that the value of an information asset to our rates over time according to an exponential decay function. And this simply means that the general rule on average newer data is usually more valuable than older data in order for an attack to succeed. Turn on attack or needs method opportunity and motive and you can remember.

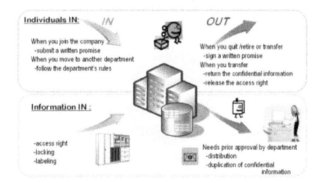

These by the acronym mom so attackers near me method here refers to the skill the knowledge the tools. And so forth which are necessary in order for an attack to be attempted opportunity refers to the time and the necessary access. That is required in order for an attack to be attempted to do if it's simply a reason to attempt an attack from an information security perspective. if any of these three items is eliminated that is if we're able to eliminate method or opportunity or motive the attack will not succeed therefore efforts aimed at preventing against attacks on information infrastructure can Target one or more of these three items. Method opportunity or motive speaking more specifically we have six approaches that we can use to defend our information system. The first of these approaches is prevention and this is accomplished by blocking an attack or by entirely closing or opening of vulnerability remember that attack occurs, when a human being intentionally Explorer vulnerability. If we are therefore able to close or entirely eliminate their ability that it cannot occur. Our second method of defense is to deter an attack and determines our strategy in, which we attempt to make the attack more difficult to accomplish.

Basic Components of Security: Confidentiality, Integrity, Availability (CIA)

- CIA
    - Confidentiality: Who is authorized to use data?
    - Integrity: Is data „good?"
    - Availability: Can access data whenever need it?

- CIA or CIAAAN... ☺

    (other security components added to CIA)
    - Authentication
    - Authorization
    - Non-repudiation
    - ...

S = Secure

Our third method is to deflect an attack and the flexion involves providing another Target for the attacker which seems to be more attractive than the original Target in this way the attacker will pursue a Target. That is less valuable to us fourth we can mitigate an attack that is we can take steps to make the impact of an attack less severe. If we are unable to prevent tutor or deflect an attack our best strategy is to have mechanisms. In place which will contain the damage to his method of defense is detection and this can refer to detecting an attack.

While it is in progress or after it has taken place if we're able to detect an attack while it is under way we may be able to stop it. But it is also important to realize that detecting an attack after it has taken place also has great value. If we're able to detect an attack after it is taken place we may be able to repair the damage, and what's more we may be able to learn from the attack that is how our system was compromised. And we can then use that information to hopefully close a vulnerability that's preventing a similar attack in the future and finally.

Our sixth method of defense is an attack we need to have mechanisms in place as backup copies of data organizational protocols etc. that allow us to quickly recover from a successful attack if an attacker finds that affects of their attack are quickly fixed. then they are less likely to attack us in the future next I'd like to talk about the multi-layered approach to implementing controls our countermeasures for information security purposes to consider a castle in the Middle Ages castles. Were often built in locations which leveraged natural obstacles in order to protect the castle during an attack an example might be building the castle on the edge of a cliff such that the side parallel with the cliff is much less likely to be attacked. What's more castles off and had a surrounding note that is a man-made band of water surrounding the castle. Which would help to further protect it from attackers additional controls included a drawbridge heavy walls with crenellations at the top strong Gates Towers guard to use Parts together.

Then we can see that the defensive strategy for these castles in the middle Ages was built around a multi-layered defense. and a similar strategy is used in information security today will use controls such as encryption software controls, Hardware controls, societal and organizational policies and procedures physical controls etc. in order to establish a multi-layered defense. For our information about owls physical controls are those controls which seek to prevent an attack through the use of something tangible. Examples might include walls locks security guards security cameras backup copies or real-time replication of data or the implementation of natural or man-made disaster protection mechanisms.

Such as smoke alarms and fire extinguishers we also have procedural and administrative controls. and the roles which you commit Ends or agreements that require or advise people to act in certain ways, with the goal of protecting our information assets so procedural or administrative controls running out things such as laws and local regulations organizational policies procedures and guidelines methods of contacting intellectual property.

such as copyrights patents or trade secrets and the use of contracts or regulations which govern the relationships between two or more parties .finally we have technical controls and Technical controls are controls or countermeasures which rely upon technology in order to help prevent and these can include mechanisms. Such as passwords access controls for operating systems or application software programs. Network protocols firewalls and intrusion detection times encryption technology Network traffic flow Regulators etc. when used together the adoption of these different types of controls. Allows establish a layered defense and gives us the best chance possible of preventing harm to our information systems put another way by defining and defend the perimeter of our system.

Pre-empting and deterring attacks providing for the deflection of attacks and then constantly monitoring for intruders and learning from their attacks. We can create an information security strategy which supports the confidentiality integrity and availability of the system. While simultaneously mitigating many of the risks. Which are inherent in a world that relies so heavily on information and communication Technologies.

Remember of layered defense strategy is best and this diagram illustrates this philosophy. Many different attempts might be made at breaking into our system and we have many tools and techniques available in order to limit the number of successful attacks outside the boundaries of our system. We can use preemption or external deterrence methods in order to prevent attacks and for those intrusion attempts that make it through our system. We then have internal deterrence mechanisms deflection mechanisms and if all else fails. And the attack is successful we want to be able to detect the attack and respond to and learn from it. as quickly as possible thus limiting the likelihood that a similar attack would succeed in the future to sew a multi-layered security strategy gives us the best chance possible of providing a solid defense against attack. In light of the competing objectives of confidentiality integrity and system availability well my friends the senate or introduction to computer security.

CHAPTER 2

IDENTIFICATION AND

AUTHENTICATION

To begin consider that one of the foundational principles upon which computers are Aries build is that with controlled access. What this means is that a user cannot say whatever they want instead a user which might be a person or a system is granted authorization to perform specific actions on a specific digital asset job as a user of a database.

For example the database administrator might Grant you tomorrow rights to read modify or delete certain data within the database. While other parts of the database may be inaccessible or off-limits are critical point to understand about this controlled-access Paradigm is that the success or failure of the Paradigm hinges on knowing example a person or system really is. That is if an attacker seeks to impersonate a legitimate user and is successful in their impersonation attempt then the controlled-access Paradigm has failed. and this is really attacker has convinced the system that he or she is a legitimate user and has therefore circumvented our efforts at allowing only authorized parties to perform actions on our digital assets in person to find is the act of pretending to be another person or another entity tomorrow purpose of entertainment or fraud and in the information age since it is systems. that are granting or denying us access to these digital assets question to ask ourselves is how can a system be certain that you are who you claim to be or in another variation of that question is it possible for a system to verify with 100%

accuracy. that you are who you claim to be tomorrow as we will see as we proceed through our discussion today for most of the systems with which we interact answer to that question is next a little bit more about impersonation which is also known as a failed Authentication.

One of the important points to understand here is that modern computer systems rely on data in order to recognize users by contrast your friends or your neighbors might recognize you. Through the daily interactions that they have allowed but an order for a computer system to recognize you. you must Supply it with certain types of data examples of light include usernames passwords biometric information like fingerprints etc. and impersonation or failed authentication attack then is successful when a computer system unable to distinguish between a legitimate user and an imposter. Because it has been proven with data values that seem to indicate that the user is legitimate. Note that we call this a failed authentication attack because the purpose of authentication is to prove that a user is who he or she says that he or she is.

If an impersonator is able to successfully convince a computer system that he or she didn't use her then the authentication mechanism for that computer system has failed. before we proceed with our discussion for today I'd like to take a moment to Define identification and authentication to know if you recall and the discussion of our last topic I Define these Concepts in general terms and we said that identification tomorrow is the process of verifying that someone or something is who they say they are what we said that authentic.

As in general terms is the process by which we verify that something is real or Genuine or authentic for our discussion today. however I would like to define the concept from the perspective of someone who wants to be recognized by a system. To and from the perspective of a user who wants to be recognized by the system. To identify Haitian is the action or process of asserting one's identity authentication by contrast strongly act of establishing or confirming that one actually is who he or she claims to be. to provide a real world example which illustrates the difference between these two concepts consider the process through which you identify and authenticate yourself to a security agent when you go through the security checkpoint at an airport, to know if you were simply to walk up to the security agent and give him or her your name then from your perspective you are identifying yourself. You're telling the agent my name is John for example that is you are asserting your identity as you probably know. However the act of simply asserting your identity is considered insufficient by security agents at the airport, and they will therefore seek to authenticate your claim by checking your state issued ID card or perhaps your passport. That is they are unwilling simply to accept that you are say you are when you identify yourselves to them. but instead will seek to verify or confirm that you are who you say you are by subjecting you to an authentication process Terraria cording to current airport security standards will require that you resent some form of government-issued identification.

With whom you interact on a regular basis then you will quickly realize that there are many people in your life who could easily obtain one or more of these identifiers and call him to be you. Simply by presenting one or more of your identify as when they are released as we saw with our example of the security agent at the airport.

Using identifier is by themselves as a means of recognizing someone is not a particularly sound practice from a security perspective. Instead of simply asking a user to go through this identification process then because I also asked users to go through an authentication process that is the process wherein. we seek to confirm that the user is who he has power it claims to be whatever methods that we adopt for this authentication purpose should be able to write reliable recognition of which users are legitimate, and which users are illegitimate and where is data that is used for identification purposes is often publicly available data used for authentication purposes should always be care of it. When the authentication process fails we can classify those failures into two distinct memories they are there false negatives or false positives with respect to authentication a false negative occurs when a seller refuses to authenticate a valid identity.

Eminem sample that you were trying to log into your email account and you provide the correct term is your name and password. And the system still refuses to allow you to log in that would be an example of a false negative. contrast a false positive occurs when a System Authentication invalid and Tootsie returning, to our email example , if an imposter is able to guess your password and they Supply your username and password to the email system. The email system will then assume that the Imposter is you and will allow him or her to login and view your emails this is an example of a false positive. The interesting characteristics of authentication systems is that the rates at which false negatives and false positives occur more often linked to each other if. for example we would like to decrease the rate of false positives, than by pursuing that you do you will almost certainly increase the rate at which false negatives occur and vice-versa most of us of course are very familiar with passwords from the definition of perspective password is an agreed-upon word phrase or set of characters that is presumed to be known only by the user and the system.

Need to Balance CIA

- **Example 1:** C vs. I+A
  - Disconnect computer from Internet to increase confidentiality
  - Availability suffers, integrity suffers due to lost updates

- **Example 2:** I vs. C+A
  - Have extensive data checks by different people/systems to increase integrity
  - Confidentiality suffers as more people see data, availability suffers due to locks on data under verification)

8

Identification vs. Authentication

Identification	Authentication
It determines the identity of the person.	It determines whether the person is indeed who he claims to be.
No identity claim Many-to-one mapping. Cost of computation ∝ number of record of users.	Identity claim from the user One-to-one mapping. The cost of computation is independent of the number of records of users.
Captured biometric signatures come from a set of known biometric feature stored in the system.	Captured biometric signatures may be unknown to the system.

Whenever you create a new password then you are essentially entering into an agreement with the system wherein each of you agrees to keep your password secret if two of your system. Are able to keep this promise and assuming that no one is able to successfully track your password then the password can be used as an authentication.

Mechanism all those words are very popular as authentication mechanisms and nevertheless have certain problems. For example passwords can be lost or forgotten either by the user or by the system passwords can also be enjoying it. I think for a moment about all of the websites where you have an account it's not particularly convenient from your perspective as a human being to have to constantly enter your login information and your password. Whenever you travel from website to website as another example of password inconvenience.

consider this common scenario with which many workers can easily identify to imagine that you arrived for work in the morning and you log into your computer tomorrow next you decide to log into your organization's website or portal where and you must provide your login information and your password again, after successfully logging into the portal you may have launched a web-based application that allows you to read your Corporate email or internal messages. and there once again you may need to know your login name and password if you perform these actions and succession over the course of perhaps 30 seconds to one minute you will need to supply your login name and password total of three times and not particular Convenient what's more passwords are problematical because they can be shared or disclosed to another entity and this is not a problem of one human being sharing his or her password or pin with another human being on the contrary.

It is also possible for passwords to be disclosed by a system if you're like most people around you probably used the same password on many of the websites or systems that you use in one of those systems were to be hacked. And your password was to be compromised by her might easily take that password and use it to log into other websites or systems. To and with which you have an account finally passwords can be revoked and password revocation can have cascading effects throughout a system.

Inside the Mind of an attacker and to start thinking about ways in which you might be able to acquire someone's password. As we can see here there are many different ways in which this can be accomplished one way of acquiring someone's password. For example is simply to try all possible combinations until we ultimately find the correct password to my other approach would be to try common passwords. that is we might use common English word or we might have seen a database of common passwords and tried those passwords a third approach would be to try passwords that are likely for this particular user we might try to learn a little something. About the user and then try passwords that might be family member names pets names birthdays, Exedra if we have proper access. We might be able to find the person's password simply by searching through the system password file and of course the easiest way to acquire someone's password is simply to ask them for it and this may sound funny but it is actually a surprisingly effective way of acquiring someone's password think. For example about what has come to be known as phishing attacks where an attacker creates a website that mimics the appearance of a legitimate website and then sends messages to users of the legitimate website trusting?

That they log in for some reason or another legitimate use other than navigate to the phony website answers his or her login name and password. and has Henson able the attacker to impersonate legitimate user on the real website note here that as we move from the bottom of this list toward the top the level of difficulty in successfully obtaining a person's word increases .that is it's much easier to obtain a person's password simply by asking them for it and it would be to try to obtain that password by using a Brute Force attack.

For example I would like to point out a few additional problems with password based authentication systems so that you can avoid them or at least recognize them when you see them often times password based off income assistance will provide attackers with more information. than they should as an example of this imagine that you are an attacker who is trying to break into a website the website ask you to provide a username and password and then click on a login button if the information that you provided is incorrect the website might generate an error message. Which says the user name that you entered is invalid or alternatively the password that you entered is invalid. What's think more carefully about what this information means to an attacker if the attacker knows that the system will tell him whether or not a particular username is valid and he can use that information try different possible combinations. Until he finds a valid or legitimate URL from a security perspective a much better error message would be one which reads the username or password that you entered is invalid.

Attacker could gain no real Advantage from this sort of air about me. because all he would know is that either the username is invalid the password is invalid or perhaps both are invalid the system is not specific role and him where he made his error and in that way is more secure another example of our charity. Mistake with respect to these authentication systems is for an organization to make its password standards probably available. For example imagine that an organization has a policy in which a password must have characters long must contain at least one letter and one number and cannot contain any special characters further assume that this password standard is public are available on the organization's website.

Because this information is available to a potential attacker it is vastly reduces the amount of work that would attack or has to do. And what are just successfully break into the system. and this example if we're told that password must be exactly 8 characters long and cannot contain any special characters try and we have no need to search for passwords of length 2 3 4 5 6 or 7 or 4 passwords of length 9 10 11 etc. furthermore designing a Brute Force attack we would have no need to include special characters in our passwords or any other of them since a standard English keyboard contains 32 special characters or 33 special characters on space key. Then by eliminating these 32 or 33 special characters where they're able to vastly reduce the password search space we'll talk about a few different types of approaches to cracking passwords beginning with a dictionary attack to begin. Consider that those are words used by humans are not random sequences of characters in numbers but instead are combinations of normal words Proper names acronyms. And so forth reason for this is that human beings have a great deal of difficulty in remembering random sequences role of numbers and letters.

Instead we commonly used passwords such as Betty 23 or chocolate frog or some other combination of regular words problems acronyms numbers etc. recognizing that humans behave in this way to writing a password does not necessarily require a Brute Force attack and still use something called a dictionary attack. Now a dictionary attack is central air instead of trying all possible combinations of characters. We instead use an intelligently designed the lifter is Apple passwords in order to break into an account although the name dictionary attack suggests that the items in the list come from a dictionary saying English language dictionary. that term is actually a little misleading although the list could certainly contain all of the normal words that one would find their regular dictionary most dictionary attacks also use additional items such as proper names of celebrities acronyms list of common passwords etc. even a very large list might only contain a few million possibilities. which as we will see as many orders of magnitude less than say a Brute Force attack another approach to cracking a password is not assemble a set of passwords that are likely for a specific user and this attack is predicated on the notion that each unique person who has characteristics that can be used to make their password easy to guess that is if an attacker invest the time to learn a little bit about Charlie he or she is much more likely to be able to guess your password.

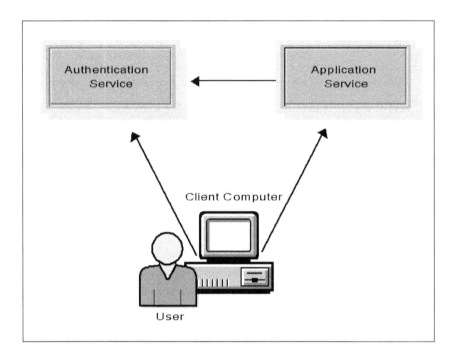

Consider this question or any of your passwords related to your life your interests your personal preferences Trials of personal details that are useful for cracking passwords include things such as your family members maybe your children's names are your parents names or your spouse's name birthdays maybe the names of your pets to my favorite television shows favorite foods numbers where's your first car something to ride from one of your hot. And so forth and it's with a dictionary attack if we gather enough personal information about a Target. We can use that information to vastly reduce the surface when attempting to identify the password of the very troubling Trend that has been noted by Security Experts of late is that much of this personal information is now voluntarily disclosed by people on their social networking pages.

But if a person has not properly configured their privacy settings and these types of personal details are publicly available password cracker could easily gather those details and use them in an effort to correct that person's password after analyzing the password of a very large number of people researchers were able to assemble this pie chart. which something very important and very scary about the current status of password usage in the world And should I charge 2% or about one out of every 50 passwords uses only two characters what's more 14% of all power. I will use only three characters and additional 14% of all passwords used for characters. But with the additional constraint that all four characters are letters 22% of all passwords used 5 letters.

Where all of those letters are of the same case so whatever case are all lower case for example 19% of passwords used 6 lower case letters. what will further 15% of all passwords are comprised simply of words in the dictionary or in a list of names together than all of these groups total to 86% of all of the passwords used by human beings. From a security perspective this is quite depressing. Because even with modest computational capabilities this means that 26% or nearly nine out of every ten passwords could be cracked in a relatively short period of time. Simply by using the information shown here tomorrow next let's talk about a Brute Force attack now a Brute Force attack.

Which is also called an exhaustive attack and pull strategy in which we use a computer to try every possible combination of characters until the crowds found. one of the most interesting traits of a Brute Force attack is that if the target system has no way of detecting or preventing a Brute Force attack then given enough time the attack. Will always be successful but I was given enough time we will always be able to find the correct password the question. Then is precisely how much time will be required and the answer to that question depends in large arm up on the length of the password.

As an example consider that if a password is between 1 and 8 characters long and is comprised of upper or lower case letters. that is we have 26 letters in the English language upper and lower case gives is 52 possibilities for letters and we add numbers to the set of possibilities there are 10 possible numbers 0 through 9 and characters on English keyboard we have 32 special characters if we do not count the space, and in total we have 94 possible symbols that might be used in a password since we stated that the password is between 1 and 8 characters long time we can calculate the number of possibilities by taking 94 to the first power + 94 to the second Trial pack and power + 94 to the third power and so on and so forth up to 94 to the 8th power in the results of this calculation is about 6.1 x 10 to the 5th power possible passwords. And this indeed is a very large number of passwords from the statistical perspective note that we will crack the password on average after having fried half of the possibilities just to impress upon you the nature of the exponential growth of hours as we add additional characters to the length of our passwords. Consider that if we have a 40 character password in this scenario and the number of possible passwords would be greater than 10 to the 7th power which is equal to the number of particles that comprise the known universe again remember that making password standards public can be a security risk. If we know for example that a password is exactly characters long then in this scenario there are only 94 to the 8th power passwords.

So we can immediately discard everything in the set below and above that that's making the search space much smaller note that password based security can be enhanced through a well-designed authentication system. as an example the system might be designed such that after an incorrect password has been provided 3 times in a row the system might lock the user's account there by requiring that the system administrator manually reset the password has a less stringent but still extremely effective strategy each failed login attempt can be intentionally. accompany you don't know for example if after each failed login attempt the program or simply instruct the thread to sleep for 5 seconds then at most only 12 login attempts can be made to help with this sort of strategy testing trillions are hundreds of trillions of possible combinations is simply invisible force attack would simply require too much time in order to be worthwhile. when thinking about ventilation mechanisms consider that all authentication mechanisms Use different combinations of just three things in order to establish a user's identity and authentication mechanism might use some of the user knows this for example could be a password or personal identification number my mother's maiden name etc.

2nd and authentication mechanism might be something that the user has that is a physical key and ID badge driver's license security token etc., 3rd and authentication mechanism might rely upon something that the user is. For example it might use recognition or Biometrics to identify a specific human being and if we want to improve the strength of our authentication process we can simply combine two or more of these authentication mechanisms. in the past we've seen rapid growth in the use of biometric authentication to take a few minutes to discuss Biometrics and their implications for authentication systems probably speaking Biometrics involves the use of a physical or biological characteristic of a human body in order to authenticate a user and this mechanism of authentication is predicated upon the assumption that the characters are measured is unique to each human body examples of physical or biological characteristics are used for authentication include things such as fingerprints, voice recognition, retinal scans, face recognition and recognition DNA etc.

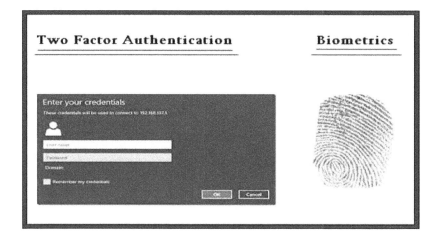

A very critical question from a godly perspective is that should a government be able to require that every citizen provided with biometric data such as fingerprints or DNA cell this is a very critical question from the perspective of personal privacy. consider for example that passwords can change you can change your password on most systems at almost any time that it is a password is not permanently linked to you as a physical human being biometric data however such as fingerprints or your DNA code is a permanent part of who you are at the deepest level. And as you give this information up once your fingerprints or your DNA profile.

Or other biometric data is sitting in some corporate or government database somewhere, you have never lost a certain type of privacy and the increasing demand of governments for their citizens or foreign visitors to provide this kind of information trial my opinion quite alarming. Your views of course may be very different from mine aside from these philosophical concerns. There are other problems with Biometrics to which I would like I will draw your attention first among these are psychological issues certain people. for example simply fear using biometric devices and these fears might be rooted in physical harm for example perhaps the laser from a retinal scan and will cause permanent damage to my vision as I noted previously some of these fears are related to perceived losses in privacy in the modern era many of the things that George Orwell wrote about his imagine how big brother has turned out to be remarkably prophetic on the other hand they're also tangible problems with biometric authentication. for example the measurement devices are expensive so they're not 100% accurate and have built-in tolerances for inaccuracies these built-in tolerances can produce false positives and false negatives for the Parametric equipment can fail and this potentially might bring an organization to a grinding halt imagine.

For example a future in which your Passage through airport security. is that you successfully go through a retinal scan from a practical perspective what happens to this airport security process if one day the retinal scanners fail what's more forgeries of biometric information are quite possible. It was established by Japanese researchers that it is remotely easy and remarkably inexpensive to fabricate false fingerprints. Which will fool the majority fingerprint scanning devices but more broadly speaking in order for biometric authentication to become widespread the equipment for conducting biometric authentication must be made commercially available. This means that would-be attackers can simply purchase the equipment and how it works and in the process learn how to circumvent .it when it comes to identification and authentication in computer security than the strategy which will provide the greatest level of Security is to adopt multi-factor authentication and multi-factor authentication. We use a combination of authentication mechanisms for data as the basis for recognizing a user. We might for example combined National password authentication mechanism with a biometric scanner of some kind or we might pair a password with temporal access locations. Which restrict the times of the day in which the password will function for the Wii controls Geographic access limitations. That is perhaps our passwords will only work on systems within a small building or on machines operating within a range of IP addresses and so forth from a practical perspective. however to realize that although adding additional Authentication Two mechanisms can improve the security of the overall authentication process doing so also increases the inconvenience of those who must authenticate themselves to the system. and it also increases costs and managerial overhead. As an example of multi-factor authentication consider the examination here what use is the combination of something that a user knows and something that a user has in order to perform the authentication process in this case in addition to allowing the user must also Supply a passcode. Where the passcode is a combination of a personal identification number to have something that the user knows plus a token code.

Which in this case is a 6 digit code that is generated by a key ring based security token loser. In this scenario would be given a security token which contains something unique seed. That seed in combination with the current time and a proprietary parity algorithm generates a six-digit code. Which changes regularly in this case once every 60 seconds. If we create an authentication process in which the user's passcode changes once permit thereby vastly improving the overall security of the system and making any attempt at impersonation. Through an automated or Brute Force attack essentially invisible well my friends thus ends our discussion of identification and Authentication.

CHAPTER 3

SOFTWARE PROGRAM SECURITY

To that protecting software programs lies at the very heart of computer security. The statement does not apply exclusively to system software. But rather applies to all kinds of software programs including applications operating systems, database Management, Systems software programs that run within Network Hardware, software programs that are embedded within intelligent circuitry. And so forth earlier in our series of lessons on information privacy and security. I introduced the concept of the CIA security Triad that is confidentiality integrity and availability.

Note that in the context of software program security software program can be considered secure. If it enforces or provides for these three elements of the security Triad further it's important to realize that ensuring software program security is a very difficult task. There are at least four reasons for this first implementing program security off and causes problems with respect to the usefulness or performance of a software program. Second and this is a critically important point to understand it is essentially impossible to ensure that a software program does only what it is designed to do. And nothing more although it is relatively straightforward to determine. Whether a program can perform all of the tasks it was designed to perform guaranteeing that the program will perform only those tasks. and that it cannot perform any other tasks is virtually impossible third the techniques that are used in programming and software engineering are changing and evolving faster than computer security techniques. And this means that computer security methods will always lag behind contemporary programming and software engineering methods finally software program security is difficult. Because even a single flaw can be catastrophic from a security perspective a software program May Implement 1000 different functions and 999 of those functions might be perfectly secure. The one function which contains a security flaw however might still make the user or the entire system susceptible to a disastrous security attack.

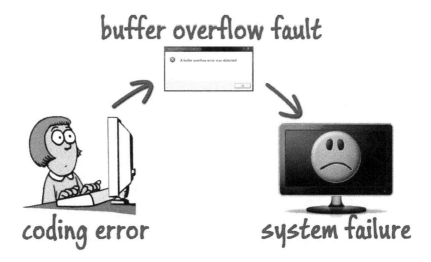

Before we proceed further I would like to briefly discuss a few terms related to fault tolerance. for some of these is the term error in the context of fault tolerance. And error is a mistake and a software program that may lead to a fault a fault then is a situation in which the behavior of a computer program deviates from its intended Behavior. If left unchecked a fault can lead to a failure which is a system malfunction. That is caused by a fault in order to clarify the relationship among errors faults and failures consider.

The following example imagine that a programmer makes an error in her code when the code is executed the air generates a buffer overflow fault the buffer overflow fault then causes. The system to crash that is it causes a failure note that we can classify faults into two separate groups. According to the manner and frequency with which they appear permanent faults are those faults which occur every time the program is executed well transient faults are those faults. Which occur only intermittently transient Faults Are of course almost always much more difficult to diagnose than permanent faults?

Next I'd like to talk about a series of common vulnerabilities that can appear within software program. First among these is a vulnerability known as incomplete mediation incomplete mediation or incomplete checking is a situation in which sensitive data exists in an exposed uncontrolled condition. And aren't subject to manipulation by a malicious user it's important to realize that incomplete mediation is usually inadvertent. That is it is usually not malicious. But it nevertheless can have serious security consequences for a software program. As an example of incomplete mediation imagine that this URL is generated by a client's browser during an online purchase, noticed that sensitive information including the customer ID the part number the quantity ordered. the item price the shipping cost and the purchase total are all contained in the URL query string now imagine that a malicious user edits the URL directly changing the item price, and the total cost is shown here when the user instructs her web browser to load this URL the maliciously modified values are sent to the server. If the server failed to verify the price of the item and it will accept $25 is the total cost and including shipping. The user would have purchased 20 of item 55 a for just $25 as opposed to the legitimate. total of $205 unchecked or invalidated data therefore represent a serious vulnerability to computer software programs to help eliminate such vulnerabilities.

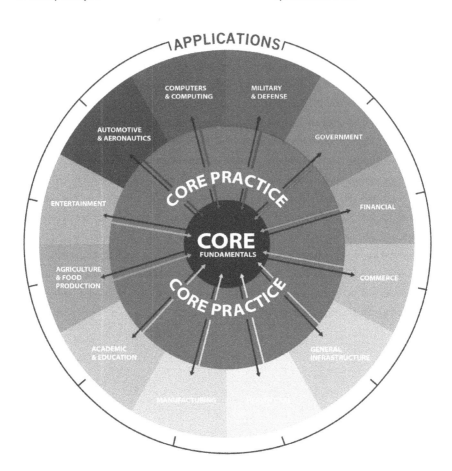

It is necessary to anticipate and complete mediation problems and design software programs. Such that they rigorously check and validate input data this can be accomplished in part. By relying upon the server to compute sensitive values such as the total amount due for an online purchase.

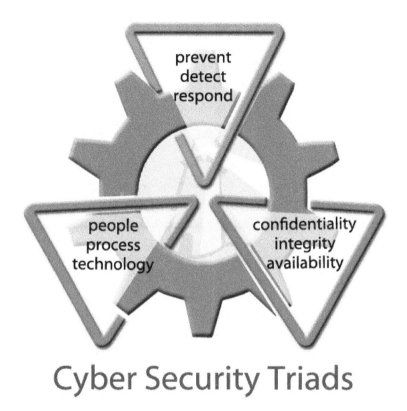

Cyber Security Triads

Another strategy is to use software or website development controls such as drop-down boxes radio buttons. And calendar controls that prevent users from editing input values directly finally. It is critically important to check the validity of data values after they are received from the client. From an information security perspective it is very poor practice to rely exclusively on client-side validation the next common software program vulnerability. That I would like to discuss is known as a race condition or a serialization fly. A race condition occurs when two concurrently executing processes produce incorrect computational results. As an example of a race condition consider this figure which represents a poorly designed Airline reservation system. Imagine that we have to web customers A & B are trying to book a seat on a specific flight. Further let's imagine that there is only one seat remaining and that both A and B are attempting to book. The one remaining seat at nearly the same time the race condition begins. When a asks the reservation system if any seats for the flight are available the reservation system responds yes. Because once it remains for the flight at this point he also asks the reservation system. If any seats for the flight are available again the reservation system responds yes. Because once it remains for the flight if both A and B then proceed to book the seat and the reservation system has no mechanism for preventing a race condition. Then the airline would have sold the same seat to two different people which would obviously be problematical in a number of different ways. The next common software program vulnerability. that I would like to discuss is known as a time of check time of use or to get to you phone her ability this phone or ability occurs .when the values are changed between the time that the software program checks or validates the data values and the time that the program actually uses those values to perform a task.

Examine a real designer handbag or a real luxury watch and when the buyer pays for the item. The sales person surreptitiously switches the real designer handbags are luxury watch for one. That is fake the key to preventing these time of check to time-of-use for abilities as for programmers. To be aware of the time lag that can occur in program execution between the times. When data values are checked and the time that they are actually used if necessary digital signatures certificates or encryption can be used to block data values.

After they have been validated such that it becomes impossible for a malicious party to modify those values. Before they are actually used by the software program the final common software program vulnerability. That I would like to discuss is known as an undocumented access point. Also known as a back door or a trapdoor this phone rebuilding occurs when a method of accessing or manipulating internal values. Within software program exists that circumvents or sidesteps the program's usual security mechanisms undocumented access points are often artifacts of the system development process. It is quite common for programmers to create these back doors in order to facilitate the testing or debugging of the program. While it is still under development unless these undocumented access points are removed from the final version of the program. However they can cause very serious problems from the perspective of program security in general flaws and software programs can be classified into two broad categories intentional flaws and unintentional or inadvertent flaws.

Intentional flaws are those flaws which are introduced into the software program on purpose by Developers he's intentional flaws can be either malicious or non-malicious. Depending upon whether the intent of the developer is to cause harm or not unintentional or inadvertent laws. By contrast are not introduced into the software program on purpose but nevertheless exists. And therefore represent a security risk it is important to note that inadvertence laws are not only commonly more numerous. Than intentional flaws but they also commonly cause just as much damage as intentional flaws inadvertent software. Program flaws can exist in many forms including validation errors domain errors serialization or aliasing errors. Inadequate identification and authentication boundary condition violations or any number of other exploitable logic errors. Next I'd like to discuss a countermeasure which is been used for many decades in an address software programs laws.

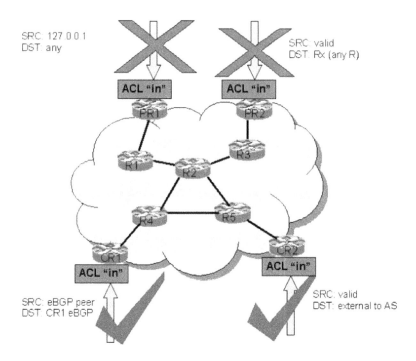

But which over time has come to be recognized by many security guards has largely ineffective this countermeasure known as penetrate and Patch is a method of acquiring security of a software program. In which a specialized team known as the red team or a tiger team intentionally tries to crack or break the software program to the theory underlying this approach is. that if a program is able to withstand the attacks of the tiger team security of the program must be reasonably sound in reality however this theory is rarely true one of the reasons for the failure of To do. Writing patch approach is that the developers of a software program will off and tried to quickly fix the problems. That have been discovered by the Twilight put simply replying quick patches to program flaws often causes new faults to emerge. This is commonly due to an hour or stress that is placed on developers due to the discovery of a fly. When a fly has detected software developers off and focus on the fault itself rather than the broader context in which the fault appears.

Finally the security overhead that is wired in order to patch a program called may not be allowed in light of the system's performance. Requirements for these reasons the penetrate and Patch method should be abandoned in favor of a more holistic approach. Which seeks to Control software program threats by considering security issues? Throughout the entire software development process. As a process software program involves many different tasks including requirements analysis design implementation testing review documentation and maintenance. And so forth security concerns permeate and interconnect all of these tasks. And therefore must be actively considered throughout each phase of the software development life cycle. Also know that because these tests are rarely carried out by a single person the social relationships. Those exist among the developers of a software program to have a substantial impact on the program's security in light of the interconnected nature of the task. That must be carried out in order to design and Implement a software program controlling against program rights can be most effectively accomplished by considering security issues. To ongoing basis throughout the entire software development process tomorrow for another way rather than waiting until the testing phase of the software development life cycle before efforts are taken to identify and correct flaws. In software program a much more effective strategy toward ensuring program security.

Still actively think about and Implement security mechanisms and controls throughout each phase of the software development life cycle one of the ways of enhancing the security profile of a software program. Is to design the program on the basis of modularity modular software programs are composed of many subcomponents called modules. Which can be defined on either a logical or functional basis of these should be designed to meet for criteria first each module should perform just one function.

2nd round module should be small third each module should be as simple as possible and finally each module should be able to perform the task for which it was designed in isolation by building software programs using a set of small independent modules the likelihood of encountering security flaws is lessened dramatically. Because it makes software code easier to maintain and the program easier to understand a modular design also enables each module to be tested and study tonight and that's allowing the cause of a security flaw to be more easily identified one way of thinking about modularity software program design is to consider an analogy with a jigsaw puzzle just as a jigsaw puzzle is comprised of an amassment of independent interconnected pieces while so too is a modular software program comprised of an accumulation of independent interconnected modules what's more each module is simple minuscule and understand that we just like each individual piece in the jigsaw puzzle when the modules are in a felicitous fashion the result is a consummate software program other software design practice to enhance program security include both encapsulation and information obnubilating throwing up solution refers to a programming practice in which the modules inner workings are obnubilated from other modules consider for example a situation is encapsulated module is designed to compute a categorical value for a managerial report An earnest security imperfection in any one of these programs that might be able to facilely Cascade to them because of their High degree of integration from a security perspective it is much less likely that a security imperfection in one program will be able to impact other programs if the program is not highly integrated with those other programs this is what is betokened when we verbalize of John Oliver City in the context of computer security here we optically discern how security issues can be considered throughout each phase of the software development process with a view toward engendering secure software beginning in the requisites analysis phase we should consider the ways in which the system might be abused as we proceed through the process of Designing the program potential threats susceptibilities and measures should be an active part of our calculus during implementation and testing. we should utilize development implements test plans and strategies. such as code reviews which are ancillary of secure software development conclusively during the acceptance and maintenance phases. we should consider residual risks associated with the software. and we should seek to mitigate risk and further enhance the program security by amassing feedback and learning from miles one of the strategies that can be habituated to amend security during the authentic coding of a software program is to conduct peer reviews of software development a peer-review is simply a process in which the computer code that is indicted by one.

Developer is claimed by at least one different software engineers with a view toward recognizing and wiping out Security office these security blemishes obviously may be either noxious or non-pernicious when composing a product program PC software engineers can regularly get to be incognizant in regards to their own slip-ups having someone else audit their own particular can help a developer to guarantee that any unexpected security defects in his or her work will be distinguished before they turn into a master directing a companion survey can likewise incredibly constrain the likelihood of deliberate vindictive security imperfections turning out to be a piece of the product program to First unless there is agreement among the majority of the developers it has a great deal more to offer a software engineer to install a malevolent security defect in the product program if her work will be investigated by another developer for the program will be checked on by another developer the associate audit prepare itself gives a disincentive to the program were to endeavor to insert a malignant security imperfection inside the product program.

In spite of the fact that in a perfect world are programming projects would be without altogether from deficiencies tomorrow in all actuality we should expect that our projects will flop now and again the explanation behind this is just not plausible to test a product program with each conceivable blend of qualities consider for instance even an extremely basic programming project, for example, a number cruncher application notwithstanding the near Simplicity of such an application we could Supply it with a practically vast assortment of information values that is making thorough testing basically unimaginable since it is essentially not attainable program utilizing each conceivable mix of info qualities we should rather embrace a procedure in which we plan our product to envision and recognize conditions and handle them richly as they emerge this reasoning is not settled in the Computing scene and for all intents and purposes all current programming dialects give instruments to catching and taking care of blunders.

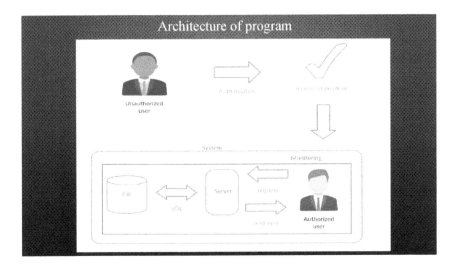

As a general framework programming system ought to be planned to such an extent that when a mistake happens any interruptions to the client brought on by that mistake ought to be minimized to the harm created by a blame ought to be confined and contained that is keeping them from spreading to different parts of the program or to the framework overall as a result of the perplexing interconnections among the modules which together include a product program changes made to one a player in a program can off and have her own inward security outcomes for different parts of the program Listen to a product program on foreseen or undesirable security results then setup administration will permit those undesirable changes to be moved back as fundamental receiving Aviation administration methodology is especially vital for expansive programming advancement ventures and for the improvement of Open Source programming program numerous developers all the while add to such activities and on account of the huge school programs it is not possible for a solitary developer to comprehend the code for the whole venture in the tail and is accordingly troublesome for a developer to completely understand the security ramifications of a code adjustment does need alternative of arrangement administration procedure notwithstanding the security controls talked about beforehand there are a few different specimens which can be actualized amid the product improvement prepare so as to guarantee that a product program is secure.

Hazard examination for instance can be utilized to uncover perils framework expresses that depending upon an arrangement of efficient strategies which ordinarily include the improvement of Hazard rundown and imagine a scenario in which situations a similar group can utilize Hazard investigation to recognize security blemishes which my other notice if utilized appropriately expectation can likewise be in actuality control by anticipating which security issues are most risky or more prone to happen the product advancement group can oversee Risk by focusing on its restricted assets to where they will be most helpful tomorrow before conveying a framework the product advancement group can play out a static examination in which the program's code and outline determinations are inspected for confirmation of potential security dangers.

Who's Fault is it?

- Finding lots of faults in software early.
  - NOT GOOD.
- Early approaches were "Penetrate" and then "Patch"
  - NOT GOOD.
- Repairing with a patch is a narrow focus and not the more important requirements.
- Patches can cause other problems.
  - Non obvious side effects
  - Fix one places – fails another
  - Performance or function suffers

The concentration of these is quite often on a product programs control streams information streams and information structures at last it is important that a product advancement has past missteps by archiving and contemplating security breaks we can figure out how to abstain from committing a similar error dissecting past oversights requires that the product advancement group keep a record of its establishments so that those plan choices can be assessed at whatever point a security rupture is distinguished preceding being sent it is basic for programming projects to be widely time so as to guarantee quality steadiness and exactness for this reason no less than 10 distinct assortments of programming testing first among these is unit trying in which the usefulness and conduct of every segment that involves the program is tried in seclusion Toronto taking after unit testing we can perform reconciliation testing the motivation behind which is to assess the degree to which the different segments that involve the product program interface with each other as proposed to taking after coordination testing we can perform work testing the reason for which is to assess the capacity of a framework to play out the capacities for.

Which it was composed after effectively finishing unit testing incorporation testing and capacity testing we may take part in execution testing in which we assess the capacity of the framework to accomplish the execution models for which it was outlined with a view toward guaranteeing client fulfilled we may subject to programming system to acknowledgment testing in which we assess the program's capacities against the Choir mints that were given by the client it is additionally vital to understand that the last creation environment for a product program regularly varies from its advancement surroundings and thus we ought to lead establishment testing and which we assess whether a program capacities accurately in the wake of being introduced its last creation environment.

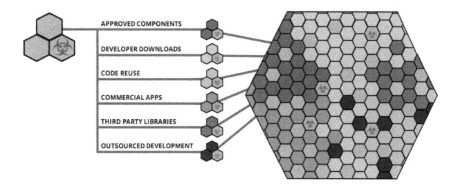

As for the particular techniques for testing that we have available to us we may perform Black Box testing clear box or white-box testing or infiltration testing is a trying methodology in which we don't consider the inward workings of a product program yet rather than guaranteeing that the program creates amend yield values in light of a known arrangement of info values by differentiation in clear box testing assess a program in light of our insight into its interior structure or plan another apparatus and are trying Arsenal is entrance trying in which we assess the capacity of a program to withstand assaults by subjecting it to a progression of reproduced assaults from both outer and inside sources at long last a product program we ought to subject the program to relapse testing the reason for which is to assess whether the majority of the program's capacities are as yet working legitimately after the change has been made to lamentably in spite of our earnest attempts no blend of advancement controls can ensure that ass off tomorrow and will be impeccably secure all things considered it is essential for us to do our best to make programming programs cure is conceivable by effectively considering security issues all through the outline advancement and usage of our product applications encouraging a hierarchical culture which bolsters the making of secure and top notch programming requires that we build up and authorize an accumulation of programming advancement guidelines potential outcomes incorporate plan gauges documentation principles programming measures testing benchmarks or setup administration norms at last however don't have any product improvement gauges won't all by itself be adequate to guarantee our generation of secure and brilliant programming rather we should make an authoritative atmosphere which underpins adjusting and gaining from oversights and which utilizes that learning to refine the association's product advancement principles in the soul of consistent Improvement and along these lines and association will give itself the most obvious opportunity conceivable of delivering secure steady and excellent programming items well my companions .

CHAPTER 4

MALICIOUS CODE

What Do We Protect Against?

Malware (short for Malicious Software) is any software program that is designed to damage or disrupt a computer system.

Malevolent code is the term used to depict any code in any part of a product framework or script that is planned to bring about undesired impacts, security breaks or harm to a framework. Malignant code is an application security risk that can't be proficiently controlled by traditional antivirus programming alone.

Which is also known as malware to begin with a definition malicious code is software that is written for the purpose of intentionally causing some sort of unanticipated or undesirable effects? Note that the terms malicious code Rogue program and now we're over to the same underlying concept. And we will have to use these terms interchangeably from a conceptual perspective one of the most critical things to understand about malicious code is that it is only distinguished from other types of software programs by the intent of its developer.

TYPES OF EXPLOITS

Viruses

Computer virus has become an umbrella term to many types of malicious code.

A **virus** is a piece of programming code, usually disguised as something else, that causes a computer to behave in an unexpected and usually undesirable manner.

- is attached to a file, so that when the infected file is opened, the virus executes
- others sit in a computer's memory and infect files as the computer opens, modifies, or creates them.

If a developer writes a software program with the goal of causing harm to other people or systems or at least problems. Then we can classify that software program as malicious. Since the only conceptual difference between malicious software program software programs is the intent of the developer it's important to realize, that malicious programs can do anything that a normal non-malicious program can do.

What the normal program malicious software programs can access and use system resources and can alter both data and other programs residing on a system. If that's what they've been designed to although many people have the impression that malicious code is a relatively. New Concept in flower researchers has been aware of malware threats for many decades Byron.

For example was described by Willis wear as a threat to Computing systems in his 1974. the defense science board remarkably many of the concerns and threats that were documented in this early reports are still perfectly valid even today many different software programs can be classified as malware with some of the most common types of malware of being viral, worms Trojan horses, zombie programs, logic bombs, time bombs, rabbits trapdoors and script attacks.

Viruses

- Viruses can travel computer to computer through a host and replicate

- Viruses very in severity

- Viruses are often picked up on the internet

Most well-known types of malware is a virus in the context of information security. a virus is a hidden self-replicating computer program that propagates Itself by infecting other options or system memory. Note that viruses can be broadly classified into two groups' transient viruses and Resident viruses.

currently in viruses are those viruses that are The only one there host programs or xylem resident viruses are those viruses that establish themselves and system memory and have the ability mean active, even after their host programs have been terminated. We will examine viruses more closely a bit later.

Let's consider worms the entire worm and a virus has many similarities. A worm is distinguished from a virus by to propagate a complete working version of itself onto another machine or device. By means of a network by contrast. A Trojan horse computer program that appears to have a useful function, but which also has a hidden and malicious purpose.

Trojan horses are commonly able to evade security mechanisms by exploiting the legitimate the relation of the user. Who runs the program imagine. for example that you downloaded a game app for your Smartphone when you launch the app to play the game, but unbeknownst to you the app has secretly made a copy of all of the information in your contact list and is transmitted that information to a remote server. Aside from viruses worms and Trojan horses several other types of malicious code exists as well as zombie.

For example is a malicious program that is designed to allow a computer to be controlled remotely by a Master machine computers that have been turned into zombies are often used by parties for purposes.

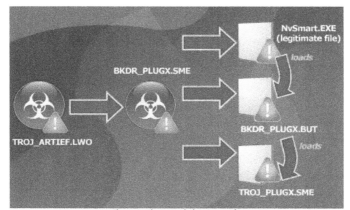

Figure 1. PlugX attack threat scenario

Such as launching a distributed denial-of-service attack against the target organization or Network next project bomb is a type of malware program. That is designed to activate itself when certain conditions are met. One of the most points of logic bombs is called a time bomb which is a logic bomb that activates at a specified date or time. It can be used by malicious parties for purposes such as launching a distributed denial-of-service attack on a holiday. or on the anniversary of some event with respect to the worms a rabbit is a virus or worm that replicates itself without limit for the purpose of draining or exhausting system resources in the real world.

Rabbits are well known for their proclivity to reproduce in large numbers. if the population of rabbits is constrained to an area with a limited supply of resources eventually the rapidly growing number of rabbits will consume all of the available resources. Turner one of the characteristics of computer systems is that they also have limited resources and I hope this example makes. it clear that replicates itself without limit is known as a rabbit trap doors which are also known as back doors are hidden software devices.

That are installed by a malicious party in order to gain syrup tidies access to a computer system while avoiding or circumventing the system security mechanisms to finally a script attack refers to malicious code. That has been written in a scripting language such as JavaScript that is designed to be downloaded and executed when a user login page script to text capitalized Phone browser vulnerabilities. or the web's same origin policy in order to gain access to private information script attacks are quite popular and have been found by Recent research to account. For at least 80% of the security vulnerabilities on the web there are of course many other varieties of malicious code at the 9 types of malware described previously. Provide a solid representative sample of current malicious code. Based threats although many malware programs are into that is they are not selective in the people or systems that the attack it's important to realize that there are also many targeted malicious programs.

VIRUSES

▸ *Is a program that can pass on malicious code to other non malicious programs by modifying them.*

▸ *When the program that a virus is attached to is executed, the virus code is also executed and performs its actions.*

That has been written for a very specific targeted malicious code might be designed to attack a particular system organization application or network. Or to carry out very specific malicious tasks an excellent example of code is the stunt worm which was specifically designed to infect the programmable logic controllers on the Siemens industrial control systems. That was being used by the Iranian government and its aftermath which uranium are useful way of studying and classifying malicious software. Programs are to evaluate that program for different perspectives. first we can consider the extent to which a malware program causes harm and we can accomplish this by determining how the program negatively impacts users or systems with respect to harm remember that malware programs off and run with the full authority of the user. And if a user has high-level Systemax have malware programs can hens cause essentially unlimited harm to a system. Then we can consider the way in which a malware program transmits or propagates itself. and we can accomplish this by determining how the program replicates and spreads malicious programs can potentially transmit and propagate themselves in many different ways including via files downloads documents script works and so forth third we can consider the ways in which a malware program becomes active.

And we can accomplish this by determining how the program establishes itself and do. You roll up system resources many different activation vectors exist for malicious and most of these exploits some sort of system vulnerability. We can consider the stealth characteristics of a malware program by determining how the program hides itself protection in order for a malicious program to survive. and must avoid being detected not only during the installation process but also when active malicious program has been detected instances of the program must be removed faster than the program can propagate itself. If we hope to cleanse the infection as promised we will now take a closer look at how computers work us call that a virus is a hidden self-replicating computer program that reads by attaching itself to other programs. This means that the host program to which viruses attach two must be executed at least once in order for the virus to spread your call also that a certain type of virus known as a resident virus can establish itself.

And system memory and can remain active without its help for this reason even a single execution of the host program can be sufficient to spread the virus widely. let's consider a few examples of virus propagation first imagined that a virus has attached to a program installer file user will hands activate the virus. When he or she runs the installer program after being activated the virus. I in all of the programs currently executing in the system's memory. From this point the virus will spread from whenever any of the infected programs is executed as another example imagine. That a virus is contained in an attachment to an email message in this case the user might activate the virus simply by opening the attachment. From this point the virus can install itself and spread throughout the user's machine.

Appending viruses insert themselves into an executable host program in front of the first legitimate program instruction in this way the virus code will run whenever the program is executed text are surrounding viruses or surrounding virus attaches itself to its host program in such a way that it will execute both before and after the host program executes developers of surrounding viruses off. and use the strategy in order to allow the virus to cover its tracks that is the component of the virus that runs after the program has finished executing can be used to mask the presence of the virus Sadder antivirus is integrating viruses incorporate themselves into the middle of a host programs legitimate program instructions thus defeating antivirus software that looks for virus signature is at the beginning of an executable program. file finally we have replacing viruses designed to entirely replace the real legitimate code of the infected program file from the time someone wishing to design a virus there are several highly desirable virus characteristics. that the designer consigner corporate into his or her virus and idea virus should be difficult to tell not easy to destroy or deactivate and to propagate itself widely and broccoli further an idea virus should be able to reinvest programs that have previously been infected and should be in machine and operating system independent with respect to the latter of these considerations imagine. how effective a virus would be if it had the capacity to infect any type of device including smartphones tablets PCS and servers running any type of operating system Windows Mac OS Linux Unix ions Android or so forth now that we know a bit about how computer viruses attach themselves to their host programs we can consider the question of where to hide a virus to virus can be hidden in many places on a computer system including the boot sector in the system's memory in application programs and Library files and in many other widely shared files and programs are arguably. The best place for a virus to be hidden is in a machines boot sector a boot sector is a region of a neuron that contains program code which allows a computer to load its operating system. When a computer is powered off bios loads the program code from the boot sector into the computer's memory the computer then executes this program code in order to initialize. its operating system and complete the boot up process since virus detection programs are application programs the operating system must be running in order for a virus detection program to be running by hiding a virus in the computer's boot sector. Then it won't be able to avoid detection 'since it will have been activated before any virus protection programs were activated another common place for viruses to be hidden is in system memory on. Modern Computing devices it is common for hundreds of programs to be executed upon system startup. if any of these programs acted with a virus the virus might propagate by attaching itself to the other programs currently contained in the system's memory. in this way even if the original host program eliminated the virus will continue to be active operating system programs or come and use our programs are grounds for this type of virus since such programs are likely to be activated often in addition to hiding viruses in the boot sector or in system memory. Viruses can also be hidden in a programs there are certain applications that allow users to write and execute macros. and these macro enabled applications have proven to be common targets for violence clever virus developers have been able to exploit security flaws in those applications in order to propagate and run malicious code.

Probably propagate otherwise the shared files and programs may also be good targets for a virus for example for a virus to be hidden inside of a data set. that is shared by many users does allowing the virus to spread quickly another interesting place to hide its code is inside digital images such as JPEG files there's an entire science known as steganography. which examines how information can be concealed many methods and tools have been developed in recent years which allowed malicious code and other information secretly hidden inside common types of computer files and these files are those good targets for viruses finally and amusingly a good place to hide a virus might be inside this reputable virus detection. Program users who acquire and activate such a program in the hopes of preventing a virus made by doing so actually caused their system to become infected in order to understand how viruses are detected. we first need to understand that viruses leave behind a unique feature which can be defined by one or more patterns if a virus has to survive a hard reboot that is around which the power to the computer is Switched Off and then switch back on it must be stored somewhere on volatile storage device such as a hard disk or a solid state drive this creates pattern for the virus. for the virus interacts with system resources in a particular way while the virus is running and these interactions create an execution. Patrick finally a virus spreads or propagates itself in a particular way that's what distribution pattern for the virus scanning programs use one or more of these types of patterns in order to detect viruses such software programs.

May scan the system's memory or it's hard with all the state drives including the boot sector in an effort to detect any virus activity on the machine turn on virus scanners can you use techniques such as file checksums and order to detect changes to important files virus scanning program finds a virus. it will typically try to run it by extracting all of the pieces of the virus from its host programs and from the system's memory major challenges faced by virus scanning programs are polymorphic virus is designed to modify their signatures as they execute in order to avoid detection note that there are typically hundreds of new viruses identified every day and that such a virus scanner. And its database of viruses must be kept up to date in order to be effective fixing a system after it has been infected by a virus might be a common number of different ways depending upon the virus and the nature of the damage that is done to the system ideally. We would want to disinfect the system by removing the virus through any infected programs without damaging the programs themselves unfortunately. This can only be accomplished if the virus currently separated from the program code and if the virus did not corrupt the program if the virus was separated from the program file in the file must be permanently deleted if one or more files is deleted by the virus itself. or is deleted in the process of disinfecting the system and restoring the system original state will require. That we recover or replace all of the deleted files this emphasizes the need to maintain file backups especially of important files without backup copy the files. That has been deleted either by the virus itself or as a consequence of the disinfection process. It will be extremely difficult to restore a system to its original state. Where infection first is the principle of least privilege this principle states that users should have access to the minimum number of digital objects and system capabilities necessary in order to perform the drugs that they need to perform a malware program.

That runs with the authority of a system administrator have the potential to cause much more harm than. if the same manner we run with the authority granted to a low-level user account second among these mechanisms is the principal of To mediation this principle states that we should check whether user is allowed to use a digital object each and every time that access to the digital object as requested Toronto we have the mechanism of memory separation. When implemented properly memory separation insurers that each user's dinner objects are isolated in memory from other users objects that's preventing cross-contamination it is important to realize. Those most single room systems such as home computers laptops tablets and so forth are not probably figured to capitalize on hierarchical code sensitivity and capability since most people use a single user account on personal Computing devices. Which has high-level administrative access to the system bacterial infections adopting proper malware hygiene and help us to substantially improve our chances of avoiding a malware infection to this end it's good practice phone up-to-date anti-malware software.

That has been supplied by a trustworthy vendor for the term for unknown software programs should always be tested on an isolated device if possible especially. If the software is to be used in an organizational environment there should be trained to recognize and open only save attachments and data files are additionally users should be made aware. That any website might be harmful website has been safe in the past finally the restoration of the system becomes necessary. It's important to keep a recoverable image in a safe place and to have backup copies of executable system files available even with all of these hygienic precautions there are still absolutely guarantees. That we can avoid a malware attack by following these steps however, we can vastly reduce our chances of acquiring a malware infection is Food For Thought an operation of malicious code I would like to discuss 7 truths about malware. malware can infect any platform for many years there's been a persistent belief that device is running Mac OS or IOS operating systems are immune to malware attacks this belief is absolutely false all Computing systems can be infected by malware.

Second malware programs can modify hidden and read-only files many people believe that if a file is hidden or marked as read only then it will be immune. remember that malware programs off and run with elevated Privileges and can easily change whether a file is hidden or read only search malware can appear anywhere in a system many of the developers of malicious programs are extremely intelligent and extremely talented and trailer and snow dark Corners anywhere in a computer system. That are immune to malware fourth malware can spread anywhere where file or data sharing occurs malware programs have no and to propagate themselves. and we should therefore not expect any Communications channel to be safe from malware turn off if it is not possible for malware to remain in volatile memory after the power to the system has been completely Switched Off never-the-less if a malware program is saved on a disk or a solid state drive.

For example in the boot sector then it may reappear when the power is restored turn around 6 it is possible for malware to infect the software that runs Hardware devices Trial positive or munificent objectives as an example consider this question would you mind having a virus hunting virus living on your system well my friends this ends our overview of malicious code.

CHAPTER 5

INTERCEPTION AND ACCESS

To begin I would like to talk briefly about a relationship between technological complexity and information security. The past witnessed extraordinary advancements in the development of information and communication technology. And these advancements have endowed human beings with an ever-growing and ever-expanding capabilities these information and communication Technologies. Not only support human beings as we carry out our tasks but are increasingly performing tasks automatically on phone Share Technologies Advance. It is important to realize that so too does the complexity of our technological devices. And technological infrastructure from a practical perspective terms means that people have more technological options and products from which to select overtime.

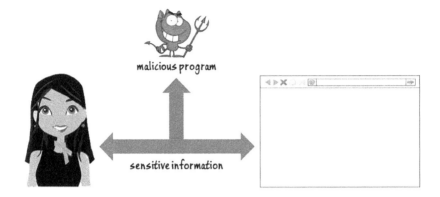

Such products provide more and more capabilities from a technical perspective. However this means that your device's software programs and Communications networks are also becoming more complex than a low-cost modern computer. for example is many magnitude more complex than the earliest programmable digital computers were built in the 1940s not only is an increasingly complex technological World more challenging for individuals and organizations to navigate and manage. but the perspective of information security and also provides attackers with more and more opportunities to cause harm to you one of the ways in which malicious parties can cause harm to information assets is by illicitly intercepting data.

Overview of Network Security

▣ Eavesdropping – Message Interception

- Unauthorized access to information
- Packet sniffers and wiretappers
- Illicit coping of data and programs

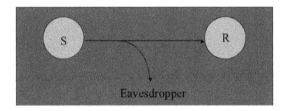

5

While they are in transit and one of the colonists methods of carrying out his interception is by means of a man-in-the-middle attack when interacting with a computer device many people feel that information is safe. While it is running is it between themselves and the application programs that they are using in reality. However there are many ways in which a malicious party can elicit the interest loan or modify data while they are in transit between a user and an application program. Or between a user or application program and with data Repository a man-in-the-middle attack. then is a kind of information security attack in which a malicious program is inserted between 200 grams or between a user and a program for the purpose of capturing or modifying data that are in transit as an example a malicious program might be designed to capture sensitive.

Time sensitive information such as login credentials or credit card numbers as they put in a user and her web browser this man-in-the-middle. Attacks are conceptually very similar to wiretapping insofar as input and work output data can be intercepted by the program without the knowledge of the user or the compromise system from an information security perspective. One of the characteristics of man-in-the-middle attacks that make them really. Troublesome is that such attacks can be accomplished either with or without physical access to device one of the commonest ways in which man-in-the-middle. Attacks are carried out is through the Yankee stroke logger a keystroke logger is a type of man-in-the-middle attack in which a software program or a standalone device.

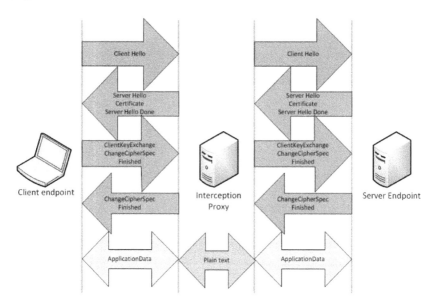

Which contains an embedded malicious program is used to syrup tidies Lee record keystrokes. On Target Computing device occasionally keystroke logger is will record all of these drugs that passed between the user's keyboard and the compromised machine. But it is common or a keystroke logger to be linked to a particular atom program or type of program keystroke logger. For example might be designed to run as a background service on the user's computer and monitor which applications are being used. When a Target application program such as a web browser email client becomes the active window the keystroke logger will then begin recording Strokes the keystrokes that have been recorded by a keystroke logger maybe somewhere locally in a log file on the compromised machine for later retrieval. Or they may be secretly transmitted to a remote destination by means of a network connection once the malicious party who planted. the keystroke logger requires the key stronger than the law can be analyzed in an effort to find sensitive information such as usernames passwords credit card numbers and so forth although the specific implications of illicit data interception will vary from case smiled broadly speaking the illicit interception of data compromises the confidentiality and integrity of the affected information system thinking about the implications of illicit data interception is to consider what sort of benefits and her crew and to whom as the result of such an information security breach. From the perspective of benefits are gains illicit data interception is intended to benefit from intercepting party in some way weather in to what extent the intercepting party actually benefits from the other section depends upon the nature of the intercepted data.

LEGISLATION – OFFENCES

> Illegal access to a computer system ("hacking"etc.)
> Illegal interception (violating privacy of data communication)
> Illegal Data interference (malicious codes, viruses, trojan horses etc.)
> System interference (hindering the lawful use of computer systems)
> Misuse of devices and illegal devices (tools to commit cyber-offences)
> Offences affecting critical infrasturcture
> Computer-related forgery (similar to forgery of tangible documents)
> Computer-related fraud (similar to real life fraud)
> Identity related offences
> SPAM

If for example a keystroke logger is used time and effort to capture sensitive information but the user never actually types and sensitive information to secretly capture keystrokes. will be of little value from the perspective of injury illicit data interception can potentially cause both direct and indirect. First Direct harm can be caused to the party whose data or information was compromised if. For example an attacker illicitly intercepted your bank account information to him you might suffer direct. Financial harm as a result it is also possible however for illicit data interception to call indirect harm as well an organization for example might see its reptiles offer or customer perceptions of the organizations competency or trustworthiness might decline subsequent to a successful illicit data interception attack publicly traded companies are very aware. of the fact that the market punishes breaches of information security and for this reason many of these companies prefer not to inform their customers or the following week.

When such a breach occurs Recently Central and a relatively small number of physical locations such as shared data centers from the perspective of vulnerability is physical access this consolidation of data represents a sizeable increase in risk for society a single physical access breach. For example now has the potential to compromise the confidentiality Integrity or availability of many individuals or organizations information assets to engender trust and as a method of combining. This increased risk due to consolidation major data centers are graduating multi-factor authentication to control physical access. threats as with other types of information security attacks a malicious party wishing to perpetrate a physical attack on an information system method opportunity and motive with respect to Method an attacker needs the requisite skills or tools to carry out the attack opportunity is also called in so far as an attacker must have some means of gaining physical access to the information system.

That she wishes to attack finally a potential not perpetrate a physical attack on an information system if she has no motive. For doing so that is an attacker needs a reason to carry out a physical attack with the reason usually taking the form of some sort of benefit for the attacker one of the interesting. Characteristics of physical attacks on Information Systems are that physically attacking a system poses economic risk to the attacker. by contrast a malicious party who conducts an attack on a system from remote location has a much smaller chance of being caught and apprehended during. the commission of the attack itself in fact the extremely low probability of being caught and punished when perpetrating remote attack on an information system is one of primary reasons.

That so many individuals are willing to engage in such malicious activities human beings are a necessary component of most Information Systems social engineering. Has been a threat to system security since the dawn of the information age more broadly however social engineering. has been a known threat to information security installation 1 ancient example of social engineering is related in the 3000 year old Christian story of Samson and Delilah in the story. Samson makes a vow to his God that he will never cut his hair and didn't return sign of devotion

Samson's God makes him the strongest man on Earth Sam's and then we have great power and influence and his enemies drive a beautiful woman named Delilah to learn the secret of Samson strong.

- Snooping:
  - ✓ unauthorized access to or interception of data
- Traffic Analysis:
  - It can obtain some other information by monitoring online traffic.
  - Modification: after accessing the information, the ataacker modifies the information to make it beneficial to herself.
  - Masquerading: masquerading or snooping happens when the attacker impersonates somebody else.
  - Replaying: attacker obtains a copy of a massage sent by a user and later tries to replay it.
  - Repudiation: it is different from others becoz it is performed by one of the two parties in the communication: the sender or receiver

Using sweet words and her feminine charms Delilah is finally able to get Samson to reveal that has long hair is the source of his strength when Samsung. Falls the song Delilah has his hair cut off that's Robin Sampson of his great strength Samson has been captured by his enemies to proceed to bind him poke out his eyes and throw him in prison where he must complete oil drain. the lesson in this ancient story is clear human beings can be manipulated to reveal sensitive information more specifically humans logical characteristics can create or amplify information security vulnerabilities human beings are social animals and as such we are naturally trusting and generally want to be helpful to others further we generally presume the activities of others to be innocent and nature social engineering then is a method of attack in which the attacker take some of these human psychological traits by using personal interactions and social skills in order to acquire sensitive security-related information Discussion on social engineering highlighted the dangers that are posed to system security by Insiders. many organizations develop information security trials that focus on the establishment of a perimeter defense with the goal of preventing attacks from. Outsiders such strategies however ignore inside that is the people who work inside the organization since Information Systems typically involve people. in some way insiders are a necessary part of most Information Systems from the perspective of information security it is critical to remember that insiders are also vulnerabilities. In comparison to Outsiders insiders commonly require and are therefore granted Morris and greater access to system capabilities this legitimate access to information assets and system.

resources makes insiders obvious term for psychological attacks such as social engineering attacks regardless of whether their intentions are malicious or benign when insiders behave in a manner that is inconsistent with established secure all that behavior has the potential to cause great harm to an information system organization that the system supports when an information security incident takes place. it may be necessary to investigate the incident in detail and for this purpose and organization might rely on computer forensics confirms a digital forensic science. That is primarily concerned with establishing the facts as they relate to information security incident when an information security breach occurs the victim or victims or government officials. Such as Intelligence Officers or judicial prosecutors term May employ computer forensic scientists to investigate the incident and gather evidence in the process of investigating an information security.

Breach computer forensic scientists seek to establish facts that can answer specific questions to all of these questions include how did the breach occur what is the nature of the harm. that was caused by the breach or who was responsible for the breach facts that are revealed by computer forensic scientists in the process of performing their forensic analysis are often used as the basis for establishing legal guilty in a court of law the use of computer forensics. Past few decades ago used regularly by government investigators and large organizations alike computer forensics is especially common in situations involving a trusted information security attack or an attack by insiders. Who often go to Great Lengths to hide or destroy evidence of their malicious activities one of the ways in which organizations and system developers. have endeavored to prevent illicit access to data is by adopting a strategy of security that is protecting sensitive information by keeping the information or Secret security through obscurity. Then isn't information security philosophy predicated on the belief that A system can remain secure if information about its internal mechanisms is not divulged a developer.

for a general might employ the strategy by invading the username and password for a database inside her source code thinking that the username and password will be safe after the program is compiled. Example of security through obscurity philosophy is the all non-final protection that was a Hallmark of early IBM operating systems. in the all not approach access to a file require the user to know the name of the file the operating system would not allow user to generate a list of the files contained on the machine not knowing the name was considered a security barrier.

In the modern era most Security Experts are not seeking to achieve security through obscurity is a poor strategy element of an information system that are meant to be kept secret or hidden. will usually be revealed in the long run to each of the internet knowledge about such secret or hidden system components can spread around the globe almost installed the security of an information system must. Therefore not depend upon secrecy alone securing information system again trying to access requires not only physical access controls but the unification methods. as well currently the Communist way in which systems authenticate users through the use of a password this is risky because passwords can be easily shared and an information system has no way of knowing whether the person. Who supplies the correct username and password is actually the real world human being to whom those credentials belong. One of the ways of limiting the risk associated with the password authentication Paradigm is to use power on island change often as an example a system might employ a one-time password approach and there's password only allows access to the system once after which the user will need to obtain.

a new password synchronous security tokens are one method of any one time password approach that minimizes frustration. For the user asynchronous token is a small physical device that contains a dog which is synchronized with the system clock using the current time and a secret algorithm both the system and the synchronous token change the kernel word for a user on. a frequent basis for example once per minute does strengthening the Authentication Protocol another approach to implementing Dynamic passwords is through the use of a shallow well pump system, and a challenge response system the user memorizes a simple formula or alcohol when she attempts to sign into the system. The system will randomly generate a challenge value such as a short number the user must then apply her simple flower algorithm to the challenge value in order to generate the correct response. Value response value which was derived from the randomly generated challenge value of turnips. Set up password a more sophisticated version of this approach can be implemented using response generating tokens turn small physical devices that embed a mathematically sophisticated formula.

That is unique to each user when they use our attempts to sign into the system the system will generate a challenge value which the user then enters into the response generating token the token. That generates the response value which serves as a one-time password system of strength in through the adoption of a continuous authentication. Paradigm continuous authentication systems for users to authenticate themselves frequently and on an ongoing basis while interacting with the system.

One way to do this is to ask users to enter their passwords on a regular basis for example once every 5 minutes to such an approach can understandably be frustrating for users and as such biometric devices might be used. Instead as an example I use facial recognition based authentication such that a small camera continuously verifies whether the person sitting in front of a computer screen is actually on the rise user although continuous authentication can prove cumbersome or frustrated in the context of human users. Such psychological factors do not apply in the context of machine to the interactions for the purpose of machine-to-machine interactions. It is therefore a good practice for each machine to authenticate itself to the other at the outset of every single transaction one of the most powerful tools that information. Security person use to prevent illicit data access is to adopt a least privilege model the printer only privilege states that users of an information system should be granted the fewest rules and privileges Possible only those privileges. That are necessary for a user to do her should be granted further user rights and privileges should be monitored on an ongoing trials in order to allow unused rights and privileges to be identified system rights and privileges. That are not being used should be revoked in order to strengthen system security. There are at least two organizations should adopt a least privilege model of information security adopting at least privilege model can prevent up to 90%. of the tax second adopting a least privilege model makes it much more difficult for malicious code to impact critical elements of a system.

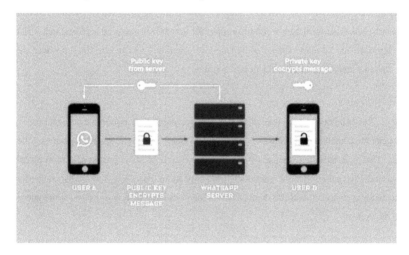

Third least privilege model prevents nun administrator users from installing unknown or unauthorized application programs. Which might compromise system security finally and importantly adopting a least privilege model allows an organization's security. Personnel to focus their efforts on fewer points of attack. if for example only administrative level users are allowed to install application programs than the information security team will not need to burn off by monitoring whether non administrators are installing or modifying application programs well my.

CHAPTER 6

ENCRYPTION

The word encryption originates from the Greek word krypton, which means covered up or mystery. The utilization of encryption is about as old as the craft of correspondence itself. As ahead of schedule as 1900 BC, an Egyptian copyist utilized non-standard symbolic representations to shroud the significance of an engraving. In a period when a great many people couldn't read, basically composing a message was regularly enough, however encryption conspires soon formed to change over messages into incoherent gatherings of figures to secure the message's mystery while it was conveyed starting with one place then onto the next. The substance of a message were reordered (transposition) or supplanted (substitution) with different characters, images, numbers or pictures keeping in mind the end goal to disguise its significance.

In 700 BC, the Spartans composed touchy messages on portions of calfskin wrapped around sticks. At the point when the tape was loosened up the characters got to be distinctly useless, however with a stick of the very same width, the beneficiary could reproduce (translate) the message. Later, the Romans utilized what's known as the Caesar Shift Cipher, a monoalphabetic figure in which every letter is moved by a concurred number. In this way, for instance, if the concurred number is three, then the message, "Be at the doors at six" would get to be "eh dw wkh jdwhv dw vla". At first look this may look hard to disentangle, yet juxtapositioning the begin of the letters in order until the letters bode well doesn't take long. Additionally, the vowels and other ordinarily utilized letters like T and S can be immediately found utilizing recurrence investigation, and that data thusly can be utilized to disentangle whatever is left of the message.

The middle Ages saw the rise of polyalphabetic substitution, which utilizes various substitution letter sets to restrain the utilization of recurrence examination to break a figure. This technique for scrambling messages stayed mainstream in spite of numerous executions that neglected to satisfactorily hide when the substitution changed, otherwise called key movement. Conceivably the most well-known execution of a polyalphabetic substitution figure is the Enigma electro-mechanical rotor figure machine utilized by the Germans amid World War Two.

It was not until the mid-1970s that encryption took a noteworthy jump forward. Until this point, all encryption plans utilized a similar mystery for encoding and decoding a message: a symmetric key. In 1976, B. Whitfield Diffie and Martin Hellman's paper New Directions in Cryptography tackled one of the major issues of cryptography, to be specific how to safely disperse the encryption key to the individuals who require it. This leap forward was taken after in a matter of seconds thereafter by RSA, an execution of open key cryptography utilizing hilter kilter calculations, which introduced another period of encryption.

How we utilize encryption today

Until the entry of the Daffy-Hellman key trade and RSA calculations, governments and their armed forces were the main genuine clients of encryption. In any case, Diffie-Hellman and RSA prompted to the wide utilization of encryption in the business and customer domains to ensure information both while it is being sent over a system (information in travel) and put away, for example, on a hard drive, cell phone or blaze drive (information very still). Gadgets like modems, set-beat boxes, smartcards and SIM cards all utilization encryption or depend on conventions like SSH, S/MIME, and SSL/TLS to encode touchy information. Encryption is utilized to shield information in travel sent from a wide range of gadgets over a wide range of systems, not only the Internet; each time somebody utilizes an ATM or purchases something on the web with a cell phone, makes a cell phone call or presses a key dandy to open an auto, encryption is utilized to ensure the data being transferred. Computerized rights administration frameworks, which anticipate unapproved utilize or propagation of copyrighted material, are yet another case of encryption securing information.

As with most areas of inquiry encryption has a trauma specialized set of jargon words. And in order to provide a solid basis for understanding encryption Concepts. I wanted to take a moment to briefly review, and define some of the colonist's terms that are used in discussions of encryption.

first time of these is the term encryption itself from crypt ion Simply refers to the process of encoding a message or encoding data so that its meaning is not obvious encryption is a part of cryptography. With your first art and science of keeping a message secure cryptanalysis by contrast prefer only Art and Science of breaking an encoded message cryptology then is a high-level umbrella term that is used to describe the field which includes both turned cryptanalysis since encryption involves encoding a message such that the meaning of the message is not obvious. We need to confirm with talking about the different forms in which a message might appear and for this purpose. We have the terms plaintext and cipher text plaintext.

In the event that you have to guard a couple records from prying eyes, you can encode them with the free, open-source, cross-stage True Crypt. These means ought to take a shot at Windows, OS X, and Linux. Take note of that in case you're scrambling records to send them over the web, you can likewise utilize this beforehand specified 7-Zip technique.

Upgrade: True Crypt is no more extended in dynamic advancement, however you ought to have the capacity to take after these same directions with its more progressive successor, Vera Crypt.

Making a True Crypt volume for your documents is madly simple—simply take after True Crypt's well-ordered wizard. Here's a review of what it involves:

Begin True Crypt and tap the Create Volume catch.

On the primary screen of the wizard, select "Make a scrambled document compartment."

On the following screen, pick "Standard True Crypt Volume." If you need to make a shrouded volume (to additionally cloud your information), read more about how it works here. We won't cover it in this instructional exercise.

On the Volume Location screen, tap the Select File catch and explore to the envelope in which you need to store your scrambled records. Try not to choose a current document as this will erase it—rather, explore to the organizer, sort the coveted name of your encoded volume in the "Record Name" box, and snap Save. We'll add documents to this True Crypt volume later.

Pick your encryption calculation on the following screen. AES ought to be fine for most clients, however you can read up on alternate alternatives in the event that you so picked. Keep in mind: Some alternatives may be more secure, however slower than others.

Pick the measure of your volume. Ensure it has enough space to fit every one of your documents, and any records you might need to add to it later.

Pick a secret key to ensure your records. Keep in mind, the more grounded your watchword, the more secure your records will be. Ensure you recollect your secret word, in light of the fact that on the off chance that you lose it, your information will be out of reach.

On the following screen, take after the guidelines and move your mouse around arbitrarily for a bit. This will guarantee True Crypt's produces a solid, irregular key. At that point click next to proceed with the wizard.

Pick a file system for your encoded volume. In case you're putting away records more than 4GB inside, you'll have to pick NTFS. Click Format to make the volume.

To mount your volume, open up True Crypt and tap the "Select File" catch. Explore to the record you just made. At that point, select an open drive letter from the rundown and tap the Mount catch. Sort in your secret key when provoked, and when you're set, your scrambled volume ought to appear in Windows Explorer, as though it were a different drive. You can drag records to it, move them around, or erase them simply like you would some other envelope. When you're set working with it, simply head once again into True Crypt, select it from the rundown, and snap Dismount. Your records ought to remain securely covered up.

Which is also known as clear text that is used to refer to the original unencrypted form of a message by convention plain text Riley written in upper case in order to distinguish. it from cipher text cipher text then tomorrow simply refers to the encrypted form of a message and by convention cipher text is written in lower case in order to distinguish. it from plain text with an understanding of these 6 turn on encryption cryptography cryptanalysis cryptology Plains Road and cipher text/ you will be well equipped to learn more about encryption as noted earlier cryptography refers to the Art and Science of keeping messages secure.

And one of the most fundamental tools are available for this purpose is encryption seeks to protect the content of a message by encoding or converting the message into a form that cannot be easily understood term. For this purpose and encryption algorithm can be used in order to convert plain text into cipher text and vice versa the basic model of cryptography involves. Protecting a plain text message by running the message through an encryption algorithm the result of. Which is an encoded or inside version of the original metal the original and encoded version of the message can then be recovered by running loaded version of the message.

Which is known as cipher text through a decryption algorithm note that encryption algorithms often rely on a mechanism known as a key. Can be applied during the process of encrypting a message or during the process of decrypt message such that the relationship between the plaintext and cipher text. Versions of the message Depends not at all upon the encryption algorithm. But also upon the value of the key in the key encryption Paradigm the relationship between an encryption algorithm, and key is directly analogous to the relationship between a physical law and the physical key for that lock in order financially viable the manufacturer of a physical lock will Mass produce thousands.

SAMPLE ENCRYPTION AND DECRYPTION PROCESS

Encryption

Plain Text   Algorithm   Cipher Text

Decryption

Cipher Text   Algorithm   Plain Text

If not Millions drawing block each block is then individualized by configuring it to work only with a specific encryption algorithms and keys in the key encryption Paradigm have exactly the same relationship the encryption algorithm itself standardized. So that it can be widely distributed and installed on many different devices many encryption algorithms. Even open source the value of the key however individualizes the encryption algorithm a plain text message run through an encryption algorithm with one key will. Therefore produce very different cipher text then if the same plan text message we run through the same encryption algorithm using a different key. Probably speaking a cryptosystem is a system which has been designed to allow messages to be encrypted, and rerouted in a particular way crypto systems can be largely classified into two piles keyless cryptosystems and Keith cryptosystems.

In a keyless cryptosystem the relationship between the planes on cipher text versions of a message depends solely and exclusively on the encryption. Algorithm To systems are generally much less secure than keyed cryptosystems because anyone who was able to gain access to the island will be able to decipher every message that has been encoded using the keyless cryptosystem. A classic example of a keyless cryptosystem is the Caesar Cipher which we will discuss shortly unlike autonomous cryptosystem a key cryptosystem relies on a cryptographic key. In order to protect the contents of a message the inside 4-door encrypted version of the message then depends not only on the encryption algorithm but also upon the value of the key.

To keep crypto systems can be further divided into two major groups namely symmetric Key Systems and asymmetric Key System.

In a symmetric key system the same P value is used for both encrypting and decrypting a message by contrast in an asymmetric Key. System turnkey value is used to encrypt a message with a very different key value is used to decrypt the message. It would be an hour to a situation in which you would need to use one physical key to lock your front door will you would need to use a very different physical key in order to unlock your front door.

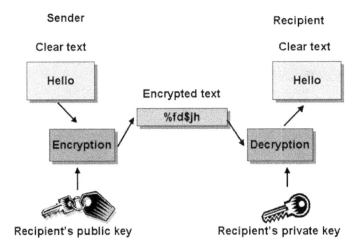

Note that in modern Computing asymmetric Key Systems are commonly referred to as public Key Systems. I would analysis is the Art and Science of breaking in coded messages depending upon the situation cryptanalysis might be undertaken in pursuit of one or more specific objectives. first I would have to know this might be used in an effort to break a single message second across this might be conducted with the goal of finding patterns in encrypted messages search pattern Island be used as input for additional cryptanalytic activities. That are seeking to actually break messages cryptanalysis might be conducted in an effort to ensure valuable Knowledge from encrypted messages without actually breaking the encryption code itself.

In the context of War for example and unusual spike in the volume of encrypted messages, that were sent between enemy troops May indicate an impending attack or a node on the network. That generates them Transcript of messages maybe the enemy's headquarters a fourth possible objective of this is to deduce and encryption or decryption key so that future encrypted messages can be easily or quickly broken.

Finally put the analysis might be conducted with the word identifying vulnerabilities in an encryption algorithm. This sort of analysis can help to design your own caption algorithms to determine, whether their algorithms are secure and reliable from the perspective of information security. It is important to remember that there are no rules when it comes to cryptanalysis. put another way we must expect an attack or to use any method tool or technique but she has at her disposal in order to break an encrypted message to one of the more interesting Notions related to encryption is that from a theoretical perspective.

It is indeed possible to devise an unbreakable cryptosystem any crypto system that is sufficiently practical to be used regularly in the real world. However I can almost certainly be broken given enough time and enough computing power with this point in mind. It should be understood as well one of the philosophical principles underlying a practical cryptosystem is not to implement an unbreakable Cipher. But rather to create a site for that in consideration of current Computing capabilities would be so difficult or so time-consuming to break that efforts to do so would not be worthwhile and encrypted military message for example may be theoretically breakable. but it would not be worthwhile to try to break the encrypted message if doing so would require many years what's explore this idea further with a mathematical example imagine that,

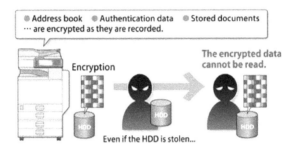

We want to break an encrypted message was composed of only 25 characters for the sake of Simplicity let's assume that the message is written in uppercase English. Such that there are only 26 possible characters that is the uppercase English letters ranging from A to Z in this scenario. There would be a total of 26 to the 25th power or proximal to the 35th power possibilities. For the message with only one of these being correct if we were to use a brute-force approach that enabled us to check 10 billion that is 10 to the 10th power to all of these per second. Then it would take a total of 10 to the 25th seconds to check every possibility as a point of reference consider that tend to the 2015.

Elections is approximately 10 billion years which is only slightly less than the age of the universe. Clearly using a brute-force approach to break that your message is not feasible with our current home Technologies. What would happen, then if we were to abandon our Brute Force strategy in favor of a more intelligent is. One which relies upon statistical methods. Well if we were to adopt such an approach we could reduce the number of possibilities from 10 to the 35th power to approximately 10 to the 15th power at 10 billion decryption second.

It would take only 10 to the 5th seconds to check every possibility note that 10 to the 5th power seconds is equal to approximately 1.2 days which of course is a much more appealing length of time than the 10 billion years. That would be required by the brute force method encryption algorithms commonly rely upon numerical codes to represent the various unique characters that might appear in a message to a simple example imagine. That we are designing an encryption algorithm to encourages that are comprised only of uppercase English letters. That is the letters capital a capital z since there are 26 possible letters we can represent each unique letter. I using the numbers 0 through 25 such that the letter A equals zero the letter B the letter C equals 2, and so forth up through the letter Z being equal to 25 Yes 30 13 with this sort of numerical coding scheme.

In place we now have the very powerful capability to perform mathematical operations on our 26 letters turnaround letter a +2. for example would be equal to the letter c just as the letter d - 2 would be equal to the letter b note that operations are circular such that a letter Z plus one would be equal to the letter A. or the letter X around 4 would be equal to the letter b these types of mathematical operations on the various characters contained within a message form the basis of most modern encryption.

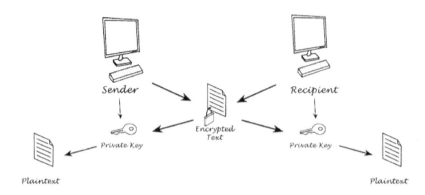

Also a cipher is an algorithm or a well-defined series of steps through which plain text can be converted into cipher text or vice-versa. Broadly speaking to her major types of ciphers substitution Cipher is transposition ciphers and products in a substitution Cipher one character is swapped or exchanged for another with the goal of producing confusion.

As a simple example of substitution Cipher might be designed such that to convert plain text into cipher text the letter A becomes the letter B the letter B becomes the letter c and so forth. The plane text me Dan would just become the letters APO using this Cipher to convert the cipher text back into the original text the process is simply reversed to restore the plaintext. In the previous example the letter B with us because the letter c would become the letter b and so forth in a transposition cipher which is also known as a permutation Cipher the order of the characters.

On the original message is rearranged with the goal of producing diffusion as a simple example a transposition cipher might be implemented which converts plaintext in time for text by simply reversing the order of the plan text. The plaintext name Dan would just become mad and AD using this site as with a substitution Cipher converting the cipher text back into the original plan requires only. That the process be reversed finally a product is a cipher in which two or more Transformations are applied to a message in the process of creating the final Cipher text.

The goal of using a product line is to create cipher text that is more secure than its only a single transformation has been applied to a message one way of achieving multiple Transformations is so multiple ciphers a plain text message. For example might first be run through 07 Cypher after which the resulting cipher text would then be run through a transposition cipher in order to produce the final Cipher text and other way of achieving multiple transformations. To run plain text through several iterations of the same Cipher a plain text message. I might first be run through a substitution Cipher after which the resulting cipher text would be run again through the same substitution Cipher most modern encryption algorithms are product ciphers.

Which employed multiple iterations of both substitution and transition in order to generate the final Cipher text the Caesar Cipher is a simple problem Cipher. Which was according to Suetonius used by Julius Caesar to ensure that the kind of important messages remain secret while in transit is Caesar Cipher employees a sub letter shifting rule. Such that each letter in the plaintext message is replaced by the letter following it. The letter I would just become the letter D the letter B would become the letter e and so forth try using the Caesar Cipher to plain text name Dan would just become the letter q.

note that the Caesar Cipher is a substitution Cipher Is found it may not be feasible however to break a more sophisticated solution safer using a brute-force approach a useful strategy for attacking more complex substitution Cipher is to employ a statistical approach to the typical methods of attacking substitution.

Cipher are commonly based upon knowledge of the frequencies. With which letters are distributed in the normal unaffected written form of language you call that a substitution Cipher swaps one character for another using. it as an example by determining the relative frequency with which characters in The cipher text compared to the frequencies of letters in normal unencrypted characters in the cipher text can be readily mapped to characters in normal written.

English and normal English writing for example the likelihood of Any Given letter being and is approximately 13% but if the letter H comprise approximately 13% of a message that has been encrypted using a substitution so it is likely that the substitution Cipher transforms the letter .A into the letter H in general terms this approach to cryptanalysis round was called a frequency analysis the visionaries servo is a polyalphabetic substitution Cipher. Which uses a keyword or phrase in conjunction with a lookup table known as a Visionary. In order to encrypt or decrypt a message.

For example imagine that we want to encode the plane text message big secret using the key word lock since the plane text message contains 9 characters not counting spaces well the key word only contains four characters the keyword will need to be run. It was necessary in order to match the length of the plaintext message in this case the key word would be extended to lock l each letter in the plaintext. and its Associated chemo are then used in conjunction with a lookup table in order to find the proper cipher text letter to substitute for the given plaintext letter using the plaintext and key word from this example in conjunction a tableau showing here will this produce the cipher text nap oboe the most pronounced weakness of the visionaries cipher.

Is it still have a comparatively short key in our discussion of the visionaries cipher? For example we used the keyword block which contains only 4 characters turn a one-time pad is a variation of the visionaries cipher that addresses this short key problem by using a child that is exactly as long as the plane text message itself. from and stoical perspective it is interesting to note that the one-time pad was used extensively during the Cold War to implement a one-time pad Cipher both the sender and the receiver of a man need to have identical pads that contain many pages of non-repeating characters for our purposes.

Let's assume that the one-time pad has 500 controller page if the sender wanted to encode a 3000 character message she would just need to use 6 pages are in order to have a non-repeating key. whose length match the length of the plane text message the center would then include each of the three thousand letters in the message using its corresponding letter from the 3000 character key and a little after encoding the message. she would then destroy the six pages from the one-time pad and transmit the message upon receiving a coded message the receiver would use the same six pages from her matching one-time pad to code the message. After which the pages would be removed from the pad and destroyed the major advantage of using a one-time pad is that the key is random and always changing.

An exclusive or operation in order to generate the next cipher text character combining each scientist character with its corresponding random key number using the same Boolean exclusive. or operation will restore the original plan text to note that if the numbers that are used as the key in a vernal cipher are truly rare and non-repeating. then there is no way to determine how a particular plant text character wasn't ciphered put another way if a truly random series of numbers is used as the key is theoretically Unbreakable avenue approach is the only known theoretically unbreakable.

Cipher lifesaver is also a variation of a one-time pad rather than using a specially generated series of random numbers as the key. however a book Cipher instead uses a book, or another form of printed media such as a poem a piece of music a newspaper a phone book or so forth as a source of rosters for the key beginning at a predetermined point in the book the letters in the book are used just like a one-time pad, as an example imagine that we would code the message agent 133 tonight at 10 o'clock near Ponte To.

Now imagine that we have a range to use the novel A Tale of Two Cities by Charles Dickens as the encryption key beginning on the first page of the book. The encryption key for our plan would be it was the best of times it was the worst of times books by fours or convenient insofar as books are readily available and can be easily replaced. If lost or confiscate her further a person carrying a book would likely be seen by a law enforcement officer as much less suspicious as a person. Who is apprehended with a secret pad that contains page after page of random characters unfortunately written media have predictable statistical properties, Trial and this makes a message and coded using a book Cipher easier to break.

Than if the same message were encoded using a series of random characters what's more a third party who's the star. That I'm excited for is being used may be able to easily acquire a copy of the key book which would prevent obvious problems for the security of an encoded message recall that a transposition cipher is an algorithm. Which rearranges the order of the letters that appear in a plain text message a columnar transposition Cipher is a transposition cipher that works by transit was in the plain text of a message. Into several columns the cipher text version of the message is then produced by reading the resulting rows in sequence from left to right.

For example imagine that we begin with the plaintext secret and that we transpose the plain text into two columns the result would be one column which contains the letters SEC and another column. Which contains the letters ret the cipher text would then be generated by reading the rows from left to right top to bottom. In this example the resulting cipher text reset note that the key in a columnar transposition is the number of columns X Apple discussed above the key would be to rail fence transposition. Cipher is very similar to a columnar transposition Cipher with the major difference being that drowned in a rail fence transposition. Cipher a plain text message is transformed into several rows rather than being transposed into several columns as with a car transposition Cipher.

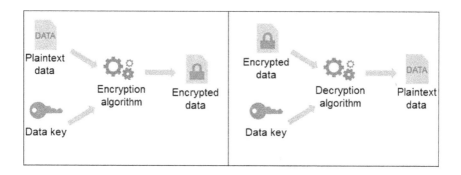

The cipher text version of the message is then produced by reading the resume columns in sequence from top to bottom left to right. For example that we begin with the plaintext The Big Bang Theory and that we transpose the plaintext into two rows or rails turn the result would be one row. Which contains the letters the big band another column which contains the letters in GTA gory the cipher text would then be generated by reading the columns from top to bottom left to right. in this example the resulting cipher text what does both get paid to pray note that he is a rail fence transposition is the number of rails or Rose in the example discussed above the key would just be too to understand the Communist way and transposition Cipher is are attacked.

It is first necessary to understand the concept of an engram in the context of cryptanalysis around and Graham is simply a character string of length 1 the set of diagrams or 2 grams for the English language what does Bahia BAC and so forth up to ZZ or personality if you have a 2 of learn British English the set of trigram or three grams would be a 8 maybe turn the AC and so forth up through Z ZZ the set of tetra grams or 4 grams would be a AAAA B and so forth up through zzzzz. Try to have a good ciphers is that the propagation of Errors should be limited if an error occurs in the inside for Mentor transmission of influences and the effects of that area should be, constrained a single error should not validate the entire cipher text finally Shannon's Criterion states that the size of a cipher text message.

Or the amount of storage required for the message should be restricted under no circumstances should the size of the cipher text exceed the size of the plaintext. From which it was derived from historical perspective it is interesting to note that these five criteria were proposed at the very beginning of the computer age. And are still perfectly valid today in addition to Shannon's criteria there are several additional criteria for a good ciphers that are desirable from a commercial perspective.

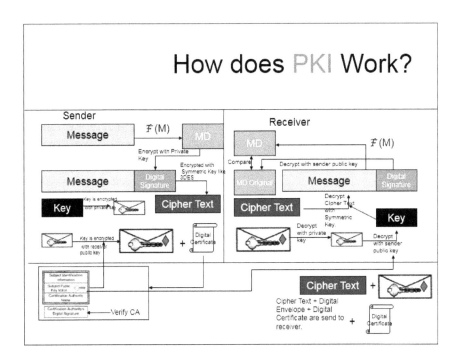

First a commercially viable safer to have a sound mathematical basis second the security of a cipher must be verified through expert analysis before it is used commercially tomorrow it is critical. That such analysis be conducted by disinterested third parties rather than being conducted exclusively by Advocates. So I would propose encryption algorithm third a commercially viable encryption algorithm must stand the test of time flaws in many encryption algorithms are discovered soon. After their release but even long-term success is not a guarantee of perpetual success one of the two major types of cryptosystems is known as asymmetric cryptosystem or sometimes as secret key encryption.

That is being referenced in the name symmetric cryptosystem refers to the fact that asymmetric encryption algorithm uses the same key to both encrypt and decrypt a message.

The key itself is referred to as a secret key and the security of a symmetric cryptosystem is predicated on the notion that only the sender and the receiver will know the value of the secret key to preserve the security of a symmetric cryptosystem. He can therefore only be transmitted via a secure Channel such as an in-person exchange or by means of an encrypted Network what are the interesting properties of symmetric criminal systems is that as long as they remain secret possession of the key provides Authentication. Put another way if a person receives an encrypted message that can be successfully encrypted using a key that is truly only known to herself in the center of the message.

Than the fact that the secret key can decrypt the message through the identity of the Sun a major problem with symmetric cryptosystems is ensuring the security of the channel over which the key is transmitted. If two parties wish to communicate securely and that work using asymmetric cryptosystem. Then they would need to exchange a secret key using a secure Channel but how can I sign or encrypted Channel be established through which the key can be shared. if establishing a secure Channel requires that both terminal already have a secret key this dilemma is known as the key exchange problem another major problem with symmetric cryptosystems from relates to the number of unique keys that is needed for large numbers of people to securely communicate to her when she was security a separate key is needed for each communicating sender/receiver pair 4 n communicating users.

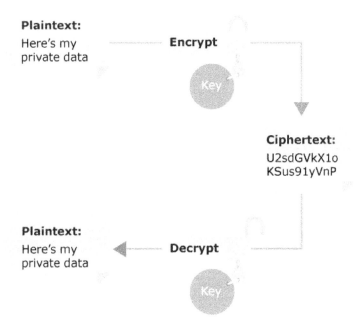

Plaintext:
Here's my
private data

Encrypt

Ciphertext:
U2sdGVkX1o
KSus91yVnP

Plaintext:
Here's my
private data

Decrypt

We would go ahead and x + -1/2 Metric he's safer that is designed to operate on fixed length segments of a message which are known as blocks in the context of secure communication. Halloween parties a block Cipher wheel encrypt a group of plain text characters of a fix as well that is a block all at once and then send the results to the receiver the process of repeated, until the entire plane text message has been encrypted and sent. As an example imagine that we have a plan I'll message that contains 24 characters and that our block Cipher operates on

800 watts the algorithm would begin by encrypting the first 8 characters of the message. after which the resulting sound text would be transmitted to the receiver the algorithm would then encrypt the next eight characters of the house after which the resulting cipher text would once again be transmitted to the receiver the process would conclude by the algorithm encrypting the final eight characters of the original message and then transmitting the final part of the site to the receiver in the early 1970s the National Bureau of standards time.

Which has since been renamed to the National Institute of Standards and technology or and its recognize the need of rural public for a secure trip to graphic standard any damage to his existing us. government trip to graphic systems that were in use at the time by agencies such as the Department of Defense FBI CIA and so forth we're not in our house and because problems were beginning to arrive with the proliferation of commercial encryption devices to not only were such commercial device is incompatible. With each other but the algorithms from which they relied had not been extensively tested by independent reviewers in 1975 the NBS therefore requested proposals for a public cryptosystem the criteria specified by the NBS for the system.

were that it be highly secure easy to understand how a publishable available to all at no cost adaptable to diverse applications economical efficient to use a validated and suitable for export there is also speculation that the government desired and cryptosystem that was not excessively strong such that it could be broken. If necessary in 1974 IBM proposed it's Lucifer encryption system became the basis for the data encryption standard or Des the problem was tested privately by the National Security Agency that is the NSA, and by the General Public in 1976 this was adopted as the us. Standard for encrypting sensitive but unclassified data and for encrypted communication the standard was later adopted by the international standardization the is and became widely used by governments and companies throughout the world.

The Des algorithm can be characterized as a block Cipher this is also a product Cypher. Since it implements multiple encryption techniques and transformations younger. than its self apply sounds of iterations of encryption to the original plain text including multiple substitution rounds to ensure efficient and multiple transposition or permutation rounds to ensure diffusion each of the 16 rounds of encryption uses its own unique round key which is derived from the use or. Supply despite the seeming complexity in reality Des is easy to implement in both summer and Hardware devices. Therefore believe that Justice may have back doors or weaknesses which they speculate were introduced.

For the purpose of facilitating government access to encrypted data in an effort to better secure their valuable data many organizations adopted a process known as double Des. which simply involves running data twice to the Des algorithm to separate keys as an example of plain text message might be run through the Des algorithm key number 1 the resulting cipher text. Would then be run through the Des algorithm again using key number to in order to produce the final cipher text the strategy was expected to double the strength of the encryption.

Encryption & Key Management

But later details so that this was not true on the contrary it was concluded by researchers that running data twice through the Des algorithm provided only slightly better security than running to the algorithm just once naturally. This led security Personnel to wonder what would happen. If they do we run through the Des algorithm three times a process known as triple d e f.

After detailed analysis triple Des was found to effectively dealing from the original 56 bits - 112 bits. I keep this link is quite strong even for today's fastest computers for data much harder to break in the modern era the Des algorithm can at best be considered only somewhat secure the first successful attack on the algorithm in 1997 required 3500 computers. For months and a lot of cooperation the 1998 attack took only 4 days but required special-purpose hardware.

It was very expensive the 2008 attack show that Des could be easily defeated with inexpensive commercially available Hardware. Thus demonstrating that both single and double Des must now be considered a sexually insecure since triple D as effectively doubles the Des key length from 56 to 112 bits cracking triple Des is still considered to be beyond the capabilities of modern commercially available systems are nevertheless.

in 1995 the US government began laying the groundwork for a new stronger encryption standard despite the fact that Des had not yet been officially cracked at the time it was speculated .by some that the search for a stronger standard emerged in reaction to evidence that us adversaries could not easily break the original Des Cipher 97 the National Institute of Standards and technology and is he requested proposals for a new encryption standard criteria for the new standard included. That become the algorithm must be unclassified and publicly disclosed further the algorithm had to be royalty-free we ride had to implement asymmetric block Cipher. That would operate on 128-bit blocks of data and had to be usable with keys.

That were 128 192 256 bits in length the response to the request for proposals was robust and the 1998 15 algorithms were selected as semi-final after further analysis of the semifinalists five finalists were selected in 1999. Including Tamar's algorithm by IBM the rc6 algorithm by RSA Laboratories the retinal algorithm by Joan Damon and Vincent Ryman the serpent algorithm by Ross and Rachel IBM. And Lars Knudsen and the two fish algorithm by Bruce Schneider and his colleagues the five finalists our rooms were subjected to extensive evaluation and scrutiny in both public and private Arenas.

To three key criteria by which the finalists algorithms were evaluated included security efficiency of operation and the ease with which the algorithm could be implemented in summer is used to provide confusion extra shift transposition is used to provide diffusion the algorithm. Then mix his columns which provides both confusion and if you go after which around he is used to provide further confusion.

Note that the column mixing step is omitted in the final round the 80s room is still rather new so it can not yet claimed to have stood the test of time nevertheless he has undergone intensive cryptanalysis by both the US government and independent experts. Further of them have no ties to the NSA or other US government agencies which terms and suspicions. that the algorithm may contain a back door finally the AES algorithm has a solid mathematical basis despite really simple Transformations that are applied during each round of encryption with respect to the security of the AES algorithm a related key attack has been developed.

Which can break 9 rounds of 256-bit AES encryption but since the 80s algorithm uses 14 rounds of encryption in the context of a 250 IT Still Remains secure. At present the best known algorithm could theoretically recover a 256-bit AES key using two to the 250 drone operations. which is approximately equal to 2.9×10 to the 76th power operations at 10 billion operations per second it would take approximately 9.2×10 to the 15th power years to break the code.

This equates to trillions of trillions of times more time that has passed since the beginning of the universe.

THANK YOU

www.ingramcontent.com/pod-product-compliance
Lightning Source LLC
Chambersburg PA
CBHW070843070326
40690CB00009B/1680